FRANK MOORE CROSS

CONVERSATIONS WITH A BIBLE SCHOLAR

FRANK MOORE CROSS

CONVERSATIONS WITH
A BIBLE SCHOLAR

HERSHEL SHANKS

EDITOR

BIBLICAL ARCHAEOLOGY SOCIETY
WASHINGTON, DC

The Biblical Archaeology Society would like to thank Carol R. Arenberg, Judith Wohlberg, Laurie Andrews, Sean O'Brien, Steven Feldman, Suzanne Singer and Coleta Aranas-Campanale for preparing this book for publication.

The conversations in chapters 1, 2 and 3 took place at the home of Professor Cross in Lexington, Massachusetts, on November 7 and 8, 1991, and were published in *Bible Review* 8:4, 8:5 and 8:6 (1992). The conversations in chapters 4 and 5 took place at Professor Cross's home on April 13, 1993.

Library of Congress Cataloging-in-Publication Data

Cross, Frank Moore.
    Frank Moore Cross: conversations with a Bible scholar / Hershel Shanks, editor.
    p. cm.
    Includes index.
    ISBN 1-880317-18-4
    1. Judaism—History—To 70 A.D. 2. Bible. O.T.—History of Biblical events.
3. Alphabet—History. 4. Inscriptions, Ancient—Middle East. 5. Dead Sea Scrolls—Criticism,
interpretation, etc. 6. Cross, Frank Moore—Interviews. I. Shanks, Hershel.
II. Title. BM165.C76 1994
    296-dc20   94-3713
                                                          CIP

CONTENTS

94702

INTRODUCTION

My favorite way to learn is by asking questions of a great scholar. That is why I so much enjoyed doing this book.

But calling Frank Cross a great scholar is an understatement. Having held the Hancock chair at Harvard (the third oldest endowed chair in the country) for 35 years, he is generally regarded by his colleagues with awe. The breadth of his scholarship, as I suggest in our preliminary conversation, brings to mind a colossus of learning of an earlier generation, William F. Albright. Cross's scholarly interests extend from the origins of Israel to the Dead Sea Scrolls, from the history of the alphabet to the history of culture, from handwriting typologies to ancient Hebrew seals.

Unlike Albright, however, Cross has addressed himself mainly to his scholarly colleagues and students. He has not written much for laypeople. In this collection of interviews—for the first time, I believe—Cross and his ideas are easily accessible to a wide audience. For that reason alone, this little book is a treasure. Here, in distilled, crystalline form, the fruits of Frank Cross's learning are made available to everyone.

I initiated these interviews for publication in Bible Review *(BR), the only magazine devoted to bringing high-level biblical scholarship to non-scholars. These interviews eventually appeared in three consecutive issues of* BR. *Our readers found them so stimulating that we decided to publish them as a book (the first three chapters of this volume) and to add to them (the remainder of this book) discussions* of subjects not covered in the previous interviews. The later material is published here for the first time.

What may not come through in these interviews, I'm afraid, is Frank Cross, the man—gentle, wise, interested, entertaining and calm, even in the face of provocation. I would be derelict if I did not record what a pleasure it has been to interview Professor Cross and to work with him preparing the transcripts for publication. In all candor, he and I have disagreed about something very important to both of us—my role in making the Dead Sea Scrolls available to all scholars. But Professor Cross, always the gentleman, never allowed this deeply felt disagreement to come between us. And I listened to him with unbounded respect, even in the rare instances when I disagreed with him. Now, happily, our disagreement is history.

There is no more exciting way to enter the mind and thought of one of the greatest biblical scholars of our time than by reading—and re-reading—this book. I consider it a great personal honor to be the means of presenting Frank Cross's ideas to students of the Bible. I know readers will find it educational, enriching and inspiring—a fresh appreciation of the unplumbed depths waiting to be explored in the greatest book of all time.

Hershel Shanks
Editor,
Bible Review

ACKNOWLEDGMENTS

The beautiful design, the lavish color pictures, the fine paper in this book would not have been possible without the generous support of Frank Cross's friends and admirers. We are pleased to acknowledge with great gratitude their contribution to this publication:

Leon Levy and Shelby White
Terrence and Ruth Elkes
Michael and Judy Steinhardt
Richard and Joan Scheuer

FRANK MOORE CROSS

OPENING CONVERSATION

I began my conversations with Professor Cross at his home in Lexington, Massachusetts, by asking him if he recognized the following quotation:

> The whole of the ancient Near East has been his bailiwick—its geography and archaeology, its languages and literature, its history and religion. I suspect that he is the last...generalist with the specialist's precision in designated areas of Egyptian, Mesopotamian, Anatolian and Syro-Palestinian studies....Each of the great discoveries in the Near East has galvanized [him] with excitement, and he has been found regularly in the forefront of those who endeavored to interpret the new data and to build new syntheses comprehending the new evidence.

He recognized the description immediately as his tribute to the great biblical archaeologist William Foxwell Albright written in 1970.[1]

I told him his description reminded me of another great scholar—himself—and I went on to describe him. "You are certainly one of the world's leading epigraphers. You read and decipher an ancient text better than almost anyone else. You can date an inscription by the shape and stance of the letters. You know a dozen ancient languages and dialects. You are a leading historian of the biblical period. You are an expert in the development of the biblical canon. You have explained the creation of the alphabet. You are a historian of religion.

You are an authority on ancient cultures. You're a historical geographer. In your time, you have done archaeology on both land and sea—and under water. You are a leading authority on the Dead Sea Scrolls. In fact, you are an expert in almost everything over a period of 2,000 years. And you hold the third oldest endowed academic chair in the country, the Hancock Professor of Hebrew and Other Oriental Languages at Harvard."

Cross rejected the comparison to Albright. "You compare me to Albright," he said, "but I have remarkably narrowed the sphere in which he operated. I work in cuneiform some, but I am not a cuneiformist; he was. I once could read Egyptian. I have not worked in Egyptian for 40 years. If I have to decipher a place name or person in Egyptian, I can do that, but I don't read Egyptian texts, as Albright did. I don't read Hittite, as Albright did. I don't know Sanskrit, as Albright did. My Berber is terrible; Albright's was excellent. I could go on. I have limited myself to a much more restricted range."

Then Cross deflected the conversation. Had I seen the recent autobiographical reflections of Hebrew University professor Benjamin Mazar, the elderly doyen of Israeli archaeology? Cross praised Mazar and explained that Albright *and* Mazar were his teachers. Mazar had remarked how much Albright had inspired and "galvanized" him, and although Cross was Albright's student, he wanted me to understand that he regarded himself as a student of Mazar as well. Mazar had inspired him, he said, in ways that Albright had not.

"My relationship over the years with Mazar has been very intimate, and I have often spoken of him as my teacher. In many ways, Mazar was a better pedagogue than Albright. Mazar is at his best in a seminar, in a discussion face to face. Albright was very difficult one to one. With Albright you could not get across your ideas before he was lecturing you. As a student, I found the only way I could persuade Albright of an idea of mine—or get an article past him for publication—was not to discuss it with him, but to hand it to him completely written, leave and let him look at it."

Cross retired in May 1992, shortly after our first interview. I asked him if he felt more satisfaction or frustration at his pending retirement.

"My students," he replied, "have given me the greatest pleasure. I have always had the view that the first task of a scholar is to pass knowledge and understanding of method and the tools of his field from one·generation to the next. To lead students into the forefront of the field is a very exciting venture. I have now directed over 100 doctoral dissertations at Harvard. I have been somewhat frustrated not to have had more time for writing and research. But I elected to give teaching priority and, when I am thinking straight, I like that priority. I chose it and would do so again."

We also talked about the pressure on students to specialize in light of the knowledge explosion. "I think you lose more by being a narrow specialist," he said, "although you're safe and secure in your little niche, than you do by the riskiness of some breadth. For the generalist, there is the possibility of synthesizing, of seeing aspects of things that the specialist cannot see.

"I don't like the narrowing of biblical scholarship into a theological framework in the Protestant tradition. And I don't like the narrowing of archaeologists into technicians, which is a tendency in Israel I deplore—and which Mazar also deplores, by the way. I don't like the narrowing of biblical studies into literary analysis. I am not talking about old-fashioned literary criticism but about the new literary analysis in which you don't have to know historical linguistics, you don't have to read history, you don't have to know anything except a little bit of literary theory. Any cutting off of the air of other fields and other perspectives troubles me.

"I know that the amount of lore in Mesopotamian studies is so large that people now specialize in Assyriology or in Sumerology or in the Neo-Assyrian period as against the Old Babylonian period. These specialties have been pressed on us by the sheer amount of material that exists. Archaeologists feel the same sort of pressure. But the specialist who knows Middle Bronze I exceedingly well restricts himself ultimately from seeing any relationship between archaeology and history. Archaeology in a historical period must interact with history."

I asked him what he advises his students with regard to specialization. "Their training should be like training in law or medicine, I tell them, where you study a little bit of everything in law school or medical school, and then you specialize. I think biblical scholars or Semitists should have broad training in a whole group of languages, particularly comparative Semitic philology and the history of the

Hebrew language or, if you're a Mesopotamian scholar, the history of the East Semitic group of languages. You should do enough archaeology to be able to read archaeological literature critically. You should know enough ancient history so that you're not lost. You should be able to check a cuneiform text if you have to. In short, you should not be restricted if you have to move in another direction. If it turns out that you have to publish scrolls from Qumrân, you should have enough training in Greek so that you can bring your Greek up to the point of using it in textual criticism.

"Then, inevitably, you specialize. But you have to have the necessary equipment, the necessary languages and the necessary tools, the necessary historiographic theory to operate. Otherwise, it seems to me, you are constantly at the mercy of the secondary literature. You control nothing on your own. I don't like what comes out of that—you continue to rely on old paradigms that are antiquated."

Then we turned our attention to the Bible and biblical history.

MESHA STELE (MOABITE STONE)

Caption on page 12.

CHAPTER 1

ISRAELITE ORIGINS

Hershel Shanks: I have heard you speak of Israelite origins, but I have not seen in print your theory that the Israelites came out of Egypt and traveled to Canaan via Saudi Arabia. Is that correct?

Frank Moore Cross: [Laughter] You have an uncanny ability to put matters in the most provocative way possible. I should not express myself in the words you have chosen. Let me put my views in my words. The land of Midian played an important role in ancient Israelite history, in Israelite origins. The Midianites were West Semites and probably spoke a northwest Semitic dialect. The role of the priest of Midian is most extraordinary in Epic tradition,[1] particularly in view of later tradition, which treats the Midianites as an intractable enemy.

HS: Jethro?

FMC: Yes. Moses married his daughter (Exodus 2:15-22). The priestly offspring of Moses were thus half Israelite, half Midianite according to tradition. This too is extraordinary, and the fact that the tradition was preserved demands explanation.

Although Midian plays a major role in the early traditions of Moses' life and labors, the Midianites later play a strangely sinister role in other traditions. In priestly lore the Midianites are archenemies who led Israel into gross sin (Numbers 25 and 31). On the other hand, Epic tradition makes Israel's judiciary the creation of the priest of Midian (Exodus 18:14-27). And an old tradition records that the priest of Midian made sacrifices and joined in a communal feast with Aaron, *mirabile dictu*, and the elders of Israel (Exodus 18:12).

These bizarre traditions, one might say gratuitous traditions, gave rise to the so-called Midianite hypothesis. A major proponent of this hypothesis was the great German historian Eduard Meyer whose *Geschichte des Altertums* (History of Antiquity)[2] is one of the monuments of ancient Near Eastern scholarship. Scholars in his camp proposed that the god Yahweh was a Midianite deity, patron of a Midianite league with which elements of Israel, including Moses, were associated in the south and Transjordan, before Israel's entry into the Promised Land. So, in part, Israel's religious origins may be traced to Midian. New evidence has accumulated since Eduard Meyer and his followers sketched the Midianite hypothesis, and I believe we can now propose a new and more detailed Midianite hypothesis.

HS: Where is Midian?

FMC: Midian proper bordered Edom on the south and probably occupied part of the area that became southern Edom in what is now southern Transjordan. It also included the northwestern corner of the Hejaz; it is a land of formidable mountains as well as deserts.

MESHA STELE (MOABITE STONE), page 10. According to the ninth-century B.C.E. Mesha Stele—also called the Moabite Stone—a sanctuary was located in the city of Nebo, which Cross locates in the valley between Mount Nebo and Mount Peor. The Mesha Stele, which is more than three feet high and two feet wide, is the largest monumental inscription ever discovered from pre-Exilic Palestine and was written by order of Mesha, the Moabite king. On the black basalt stele, Mesha boasts of conquering Israelite territory and humiliating the tribe of Dan.

The intact stele was discovered in 1868 in Dhiban, now in Jordan, but the stone was later broken into pieces, perhaps because individual pieces were more valuable on the market than the stele would have been in one piece. After a long search, Charles Clermont-Ganneau, a French diplomat and amateur archaeologist, recovered some of the fragments. By combining them with partial copies of the text made before the stone was destroyed, Clermont-Ganneau was able to piece together most of the inscription. The smooth areas on the stone indicate Clermont-Ganneau's reconstruction.

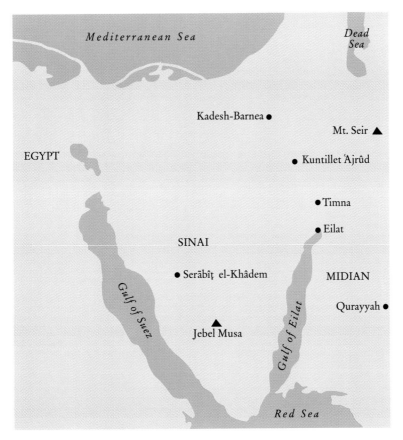

ROUTE OF THE EXODUS. One of the most vexing problems in biblical archaeology is establishing the route taken by the Israelites when they left Egypt. Many theories have been proposed for tracking the Exodus—a northern route along the Mediterranean called the "Way of the Land of the Philistines" or the "Way of the Sea," a central route called the "Way of Shur" and a southern route that passes by Jebel Musa, the mountain traditionally identified as Mount Sinai.

Frank Moore Cross considers efforts to locate Mount Sinai in the Sinai peninsula misguided. He believes the Israelites wandered through the land of Midian, east of the Gulf of Eilat (modern northwest Saudi Arabia).

HS: In Saudi Arabia?

FMC: Yes, Midian is in the northwestern border area of what is now Saudi Arabia. I prefer to refer to it by the biblical term "Midian." Incidentally the Saudis will not permit excavation in this area despite efforts that Peter Parr and I conducted some years ago on behalf of the American Schools of Oriental Research and the British School of Archaeology.

HS: Isn't Midian traditionally placed in Sinai?

FMC: I should say rather that Sinai is placed in Midian.

HS: Are you saying that all scholars agree that Midian is south of the Jordanian-Saudi border?

FMC: I cannot say categorically all, but the consensus is that ancient Midian was south of Eilat on the Saudi side. Note too that tradition holds that the Midianites controlled routes north through Edom and Moab very much like the later Nabateans, and that Midian in Israel's earliest poetry is associated with Edom, Mount Seir and Teman.

The notion that the "mountain of God" called Sinai and Horeb was located in what we now call the Sinai Peninsula has no older tradition supporting it than Byzantine times. It is one of the many holy places created for pilgrims in the Byzantine period.

HS: In the fourth century?

FMC: Yes.

HS: So you would place Sinai in what is today Saudi Arabia?

FMC: You haven't forgotten your skills in cross- (or Cross-) examination. Yes, in the northwestern corner of Saudi Arabia, ancient Midian. There is new evidence favoring this identification. In the late 1960s and 1970s when Israel controlled the Sinai Peninsula, especially in the period shortly before the area was returned to Egypt, the peninsula was explored systematically and intensely by archaeologists. What

A LAND OF PHYSICAL CONTRASTS—forbidding deserts and formidable mountains—ancient Midian is also a land of contrasts in Israelite tradition. On the one hand, Moses sojourned in Midian after slaying an Egyptian (Exodus 2:15); he married the daughter of Jethro, a Midianite priest (Exodus 2:21); and Jethro later advised Moses on how to dispense justice efficiently (Exodus 18:33-27). On the other hand, the Midianites are depicted as archenemies who led the Israelites into sin (Numbers 25 and 31). Frank Moore Cross attributes the pro-Midianite position to the combined J (Yahwist) and E (Elohist) strand of the Pentateuch, which he calls the Epic tradition. He ascribes the anti-Midianite outlook to the P (Priestly code) component of the Pentateuch.

they found from the 13th to 12th centuries B.C.E., the era of Moses and Israel's entry into Canaan, was an archaeological blank save for Egyptian mining sites at Serābîṭ el-Khâdem (photos, pp. 71-73) and Timna (photos, pp. 18-19) near Eilat. They found no evidence of settled occupation. This proved true even at the site generally identified with Kadesh-Barnea (ʿÊn Qudeirat), which was not occupied until the tenth century B.C.E. at the earliest. The fortress was constructed only in the ninth century.[3]

On the other hand, recent surveys of Midian have produced surprising discoveries of a developed civilization in precisely the period in question, the end of the Late Bronze Age and the beginning of the Iron Age, the 13th to 12th centuries.[4] At Qurayyah, archaeologists discovered a major fortified citadel, a walled village and extensive irrigation works (see photos, p. 20). Characteristic pottery called Midianite ware—usually called Hejaz ware in Saudi journals—radiates out from the northern Hejaz into southern Transjordan and

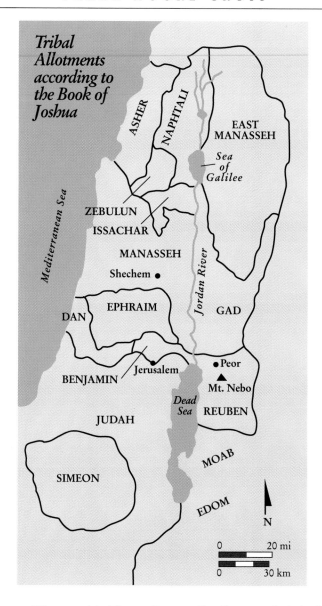

Tribal Allotments according to the Book of Joshua

sites near Eilat, notably Timna. Extraordinarily enough, it is absent from the Sinai. In short, we have a blank Sinai and a thriving culture in Midian in this era.

Biblical traditions preserve much Midianite lore. At the end of his life, Moses is described as going north into the district of Mount Nebo and Mount Peor in Transjordan. Both an Epic source and the Priestly source in the Balaam cycle in the Book of Numbers record traditions of Midianite presence in this area. Evidently they exercised at least commercial hegemony, controlling the newly developed incense trade.

In Israelite sources, this area of Transjordan was assigned to Reuben but was lost to Moab early and is often called the "plains of Moab" in the Bible. We know from the ninth-century (B.C.E.) Mesha Stele[5] that there was a sanctuary in the city of Nebo.[6] Moses was buried in this valley. Balaam delivered his oracles (Numbers 23:28), we are told, from Mount Peor; and the notorious orgy in which there was coupling with Midianite women (Numbers 25:1-5) has its locus here as well.

HS: Are you placing Nebo where it is traditionally placed?

FMC: Mount Nebo, yes. The city of Nebo I have shifted from the Byzantine site on the south of the mountain to an early Iron Age site right in the heart of the valley over against Mount Peor.

I think it is fair to say that we can trace a cycle of Midianite lore from the locale of the mountain of God in Midian, and northward to Reuben. The Book of Deuteronomy places Moses' second giving of the law (Deuteronomy 4:44 through chapter 26) and the renewal of the covenant of the tribes in Reuben (Deuteronomy 29-31). We are told too that in this same district the rallying of the militia took place and the entry into the Promised Land was launched (Joshua 2-4): "O my people, remember...what happened from Shittim to Gilgal," as Micah reminds us (Micah 6:5).

HS: Can you trace the route? The Exodus route would have to go across Sinai, wouldn't it, if you are leaving Egypt.

FMC: At best we can only speculate. A mountain of paper has been expended in attempting to locate the stations of the Exodus in Numbers 33. There are almost as many opinions as there are scholars. One of the most persuasive treatments I know is Martin Noth's.[7] He argues that underlying the Priestly document (and the list of stations in Deuteronomy 10:6-7) was a list of pilgrimage stations from Reuben to Midian, secondarily supplemented to cross to Egypt. Pilgrimages to the southern mountain are reflected in the narrative of Elijah's journey to Sinai. The small site of Kuntillet ʿAjrûd[8] (photos, pp. 24-25), from the late ninth century B.C.E., is probably a pilgrimage station on the way to Eilat and south. Pilgrim texts mention "Yahweh

of Samaria," and notably "Yahweh of Teman," probably a reference to a Midianite shrine either in Midian or on Mount Seir.

HS: Isn't the movement of the Israelites into Saudi Arabia in the opposite direction from the way they wished to go?

FMC: That depends on what their goal was.

HS: I am assuming it was the Promised Land.

FMC: Matters are much more complicated. The historian has great difficulty separating history from legend and tradition reshaped in the literary interests of poets and seers. There is some reason to believe that there is a historical nucleus in the tradition that some elements of what later became Israel—the Moses group, we can call them, or

CLIFFS OF THE TIMNA VALLEY. Located in the Negev about 19 miles northwest of Eilat (see map, p. 13), Timna has been the site of copper mines since the Chalcolithic period (fourth millennium B.C.E.). The area around the towering cliffs of the Timna Valley, like the ones seen in the photo (bottom left) called "King Solomon's Pillars" (there is no evidence that Solomon had anything to do with the site), is honeycombed with more than 7,000 mine shafts. In a survey of the area in 1966, archaeologist Beno Rothenberg discovered a small structure built against the base of one of the pillars (top left). The building is about 50 feet on each side with preserved remains five feet high, a long-standing sanctuary that was once a temple to the Egyptian goddess Hathor (late 14th to mid-13th century B.C.E.). The site was later used as a tented shrine during a Midianite phase dating to about the mid-12th century B.C.E., during which representations of Hathor as well as earlier hieroglyphic inscriptions were systematically defaced. Examples of Midianite pottery from Timna are shown above.

FORTIFIED CITADEL AT QURAYYAH. Evidence of 13th- and 12th-century activity is scarce in the area traditionally identified as Sinai despite intense archaeological exploration in the 1960s and 1970s when the area was under Israeli control. In Midian, on the other hand, considerable archaeological remains dating to the 13th and 12th centuries B.C.E. have been found.

At Qurayyah, for example, archaeologists uncovered a fortified citadel (top), a walled village and extensive irrigation works. Midianite ware (above) has been recovered in northwestern Arabia, southern Transjordan and sites near Eilat (such as Timna). The resulting picture of the period, Professor Cross notes, is of a "blank Sinai and a thriving culture in Midian." Based on this evidence, he concludes that the people who left Egypt and later joined other tribal groups to form the Israelite people traveled through Midian, which should properly be identified as biblical Sinai.

proto-Israel—fled from Egypt and eventually (a generation, or 40 years later, according to the biblical chronology) ended up invading Canaan from the Reubenite area of Transjordan. There is also archaeological evidence that tribal elements moved from east to west when they occupied the central hill country of Canaan. Certainly there was the movement of other groups of people of patriarch stock into the hill country in this same period who were not of the Moses group. In Deuteronomistic tradition we are told that the Israelites compassed Mount Seir many days.[9]

So we cannot think of Israel leaving Egypt and making a beeline for the Promised Land. If the tradition of their long sojourn in the wilderness has a historical basis, then the historian must ask how this tradition survived. Even if the group was small, counted at most in hundreds rather than millions, as tradition in Numbers (Numbers 1:46) claims, they could not have survived for a generation in uninhabited Sinai—unless one takes at face value the legend of the heavens raining manna and the migration with miraculous frequency of myriads of quail (Exodus 16:4-36).

No, if the Israelite contingent from Egypt survived long in the southern wilderness, it was because they headed for an area where there was civilization, irrigated crops, the means of sustenance. Southern Edom and Midian supply this need, and so I believe they headed there. And this doesn't even mention the alliance by marriage between Moses' family and the priestly house of Midian. That this alliance had a historical basis is difficult to doubt—since it was profoundly objectionable to many circles in Israel, including the Priestly school, which finally edited the Tetrateuch (Genesis, Exodus, Leviticus and Numbers). Yet it was kept in.

HS: You mentioned in passing "patriarch stock." Do you mean the descendants of the patriarchs in the Bible?

FMC: More or less. Peoples who spoke the language and bore the personal names that we can call patriarchal or, better, Hebrew. Much has been written on the terms ʿApiru and Hebrew (ʿibrî) and their relationship. I have long held that the term ʿapiru (not ʿapīru as some vocalize it) means "client" or "member of a client class."[10] The ʿApiru in fact had no status in the Canaanite feudal order but attached himself to it in a variety of roles—in military service, as an agricultural worker, etc. Or, since he had no legal status, he could turn to outlawry.

This client class, which was despised by Canaanite nobility before Israel's appearance in Canaan, became *ʿIbrîm*, Hebrews, a class or group—only later did the term carry ethnic overtones—with whom Israel identified and who had special status in early Israelite legal lore. Surely in the consolidation of the Israelite league, serfs (*ḥupšu* who became freemen, *ḥopši*, a linguistic development much like that of *ʿapiru* becoming *ʿibrî*), clients and slaves were readily absorbed into the nation, imprinting Israel with the consciousness of being of lowly origins, outsiders in Canaanite society.

MOUNT NEBO. From Mount Nebo, which rises from the plains of Moab just east of the Jordan River, Moses was allowed to look across to the Promised Land, although he was fated never to enter it (Deuteronomy 34:1-8). He was buried in an unknown spot in the valley between Mount Nebo and Mount Peor.

Other biblical events associated with this area include the delivery of Balaam's oracles from Mount Peor (Numbers 23 and 24) and the illicit coupling of Israelite men with Midianite women (Numbers 25). These incidents, although they took place in Moab, include references to a Midianite presence in the area. Professor Cross believes that the Midianites, who controlled the newly developed incense trade, exercised commercial hegemony over the area.

The ʿApiru are mentioned often in inscriptions from the Late Bronze Age in Syria and Egypt, and especially in the Amarna letters, correspondence from the 14th century B.C.E., chiefly between Canaanite vassal kings and their Egyptian overlords.[11] From these letters, we learn that a group of ʿapiru headed by a certain Lab'ayyu actually seized the important city of Shechem and terrified the kinglets round about, who in turn urged the pharaoh to come to their aid.

The Amarna letters reveal that the feudal system in Palestine was breaking down and that dissident elements were making all kinds of trouble. Egypt under the pharaoh Akhenaten was weak and losing control of the empire, which included Canaan.

George Mendenhall[12] and Norman Gottwald[13] have promoted the theory that Israel came into being in the land as the result of a social revolution. I think this theory is not without some merit, but I don't think this single (for Gottwald, Marxist) explanation of Israelite origins in the land is the whole story.

Israel also moved from the east into the hill country of central Canaan, a country largely uninhabited.[14] Albrecht Alt, and most recently Israel Finkelstein, have argued that Israelite elements, small groups of nomadic pastoralists, peacefully infiltrated uninhabited areas in Cisjordan and slowly began to settle down in the course of the late 13th and early 12th centuries B.C.E. This model too, I believe, has some validity, but again I find it overly simple.

The biblical tradition of a systematic, all-encompassing military conquest is, no doubt, much overdrawn, and there are some contradictory elements even in the conquest tradition as we have it in the Bible.[15] But I do not believe that Israel moved into the land without any conflict. Tribal people are almost by definition warriors as well as keepers of small cattle (chiefly sheep and goats in mixed flocks in this period).[16] And the rapid and aggressive formation of the league must have led to military confrontations.

I am bemused by the fact that, given the widespread evidence of destruction in Canaan at the end of the Late Bronze Age and the beginning of the Iron Age, some scholars are inclined to attribute the violence to various people, despite the lack of written records, to almost anyone—except Israel, for whom we have elaborate written records of warfare. The notion of conquest, largely discredited these days, and properly so in the stereotyped, Deuteronomistic

KUNTILLET ʿAJRÛD, a late ninth-century B.C.E. pilgrimage site and rest stop (shown at right), sits atop a westward-facing plateau in the northern Sinai. Frank Cross suggests that the places listed in Numbers 33 and Deuteronomy 10 as sites through which the Israelites passed after leaving Egypt, as well as sites in Moab and Midian, were pilgrimage stations much like this one. Among the remarkable finds at Kuntillet ʿAjrûd was a fragment from a large storage jar bearing a drawing and an inscription (top photo and artist's rendition), which have been the subject of heated debate. The inscription reads, "I have blessed you by Yahweh of Samaria and his ʾasherah." Some scholars have suggested that Yahweh is represented at left and the goddess ʾAsherah either at center or at right. Others argue that both the left and center figures are the Egyptian god Bes, depicted in typical arms-akimbo pose topped by a characteristic feathered headdress; the figure at right, according to this theory, is an ordinary lyre player.

version, is not without testimony, archaeological and literary. Israel's premonarchical hymns, "Songs of the Wars of Yahweh," testify to early wars and conquests.

In short, I prefer a complex explanation of the origins of Israel in the land to any of the simple models now being offered. But to return to our thesis, embedded in the biblical tradition is historical evidence of a migration or incursion from Reuben of elements of Israel who came from the south and had ties to Midian, whose original leader was Moses.

HS: Did they come from Egypt?

FMC: Moses has an Egyptian name, and tradition early and late puts him in the house of pharaoh. His descendants, too, sometimes exhibit Egyptian names. I have no reason to doubt that many who eventually reached Reuben (or the "plains of Moab" as the area is more frequently called in the Bible) came north from southern Edom and northern Midian, where the Midianite league flourished, and where, in my view, the mountain of God was located. They were refugees

from Egypt or, in traditional terms, patriarchal folk who were freed from Egyptian slavery.

HS: Do you have any guess which mountain might be Mount Sinai?

FMC: I really don't. There are several enormous mountains in what is now northwestern Saudi Arabia. Jebel el-Lawz is the highest mountain in Midian—8,465 feet—higher than any mountain in the Sinai Peninsula. But biblical Mount Sinai need not be the highest mountain. There is some reason to search for it in southern Edom, which was Midianite terrain before the expansion of the Edomites south. Archaic poetry in the Bible describes Yahweh as coming from Edom. For example, in Judges 5:1-31, the oldest of the biblical narrative songs (late 12th century B.C.E.), we read:

> When Thou Yahweh went forth from Seir,
> When Thou didst march forth from the highlands of Edom,
> Earth shook,
> mountains shuddered;
> Before Yahweh, Lord of Sinai,
> Before Yahweh, God of Israel
>
> (Judges 5:4-5)

And in the Blessing of Moses, which is also very old, we read:

> Yahweh from Sinai came,
> He beamed forth from Seir upon us,
> He shone from Mount Paran
>
> (Deuteronomy 33:2)

The name "Seir" refers of course to a mountainous district of Edom. The following verses are found in Habakkuk 3:3-7 (one of the oldest and most primitive hymns in the Hebrew Bible):[17]

> Eloah (God) came from Teman,
> The Holy One from Mount Paran.
> His majesty covered heaven,
> His praise filled the earth,
> He shone like a destroying fire....
> He stood and he shook earth,
> He looked and startled nations.
> Ancient mountains were shattered,
> Eternal hills collapsed,

> Eternal orbits were destroyed.
> The tents of Kushan shook,
> Tent curtains of the land of Midian.

I would argue that these archaic songs that locate Yahweh's movements in the southeast—in Edom/Seir/Teman/Midian/Cushan—are our most reliable evidence for locating Sinai/Horeb, the mountain of God. The search for origins and the reconstruction of history from material that arises in oral tradition is always a precarious task. The singers of narrative poems—I speak of them as epic sources—follow certain traditional patterns that include mythological elements. They do not contain what we would call history in the modern sense of that term. We are dealing with epic, which does not fit easily into either the genres of fiction or of history.

How can the historian ferret out valid historical memory in such traditional narratives? Perhaps he cannot. I am inclined to think, however, that old traditions that have no social function in later Israel—or traditions that actually flout later orthodoxy—that such traditions may preserve authentic historical memories, memories too fixed in archaic poetry to be revised out or suppressed.

HS: Can you give me an example?

FMC: In later Israel, the Midianites, as we have seen, were the bitter enemies of Israel according to one stratum of tradition. One need only read the Priestly account of the episode of Baʿal Peor and the war in which the Midianites were annihilated by Israel.[18] Moses is described as standing helpless and allowing the orgy and apostasy to proceed without reprimand, according to the Priestly source; the hero is the Aaronid Phineas, who, as a reward for his intervention, is given an eternal priesthood. The fertility rites include what may euphemistically be called sacral marriage between a Midianite woman and an Israelite man, both of exalted lineage. Phineas spears the couple, whom he catches *in flagrante delicto*.

Alongside such traditions are older accounts of the priest of Midian assisting Moses at Mount Sinai, of a scion of Midian guiding Israel in the desert, of the marriage of Moses to a Midianite woman, of Moses siring mixed offspring, of Miriam being turned pure white with leprosy for objecting to Moses' marriage to a dark-skinned Midianite. Indeed, as we search the JE traditions,[19] Epic traditions as opposed to the later Priestly source, there is no hint of polemic against Midian. On the contrary, in this stratum of tradition, it is Aaron who creates the golden bull and thereby leads Israel into apostasy, idolatry and orgiastic rites (Exodus 32). And it is the Levites, not the Aaronids, who receive an eternal priesthood for slaughtering 3,000 of the participants in the affair.

In the accounts of the stay in the wilderness of Sinai, there are a series of "conflict stories," especially between Moses and his allies, including Midian, and, on the other hand, Aaron, Miriam and their allies.[20] Israel's epic singers did not preserve these traditions in order to sully the reputation of Moses. Evidently the Midianite traditions

CUNEIFORM TABLET FROM TELL EL-AMARNA. More than 350 cuneiform tablets like the one shown here have been found at Tell el-Amarna, the site of the capital of Egypt under Pharaoh Akhenaten (Amenophis IV, 1353-1335 B.C.E.). Many of the tablets contain correspondence between Akhenaten (or his predecessor) and vassal kings in Canaan. The letters reveal an empire in trouble. Egypt was losing control of subject states, including Canaan, and Canaan itself was beset by problems inflicted by a mysterious people known as the ʿApiru, who were outside the ranks of normal Canaanite society and were hired as agricultural workers or mercenaries. Some even say the ʿApiru were outlaws. The Amarna letter shown here records that a group of ʿApiru, led by a certain Lab'ayyu (his name is highlighted in the photo), had seized the city of Shechem. Professor Cross proposes that the ʿApiru were one group that became part of the Israelite confederation and that the name ʿApiru was transformed into *Ibrîm*, the Hebrew name for "Hebrews."

were too firmly established in the old sources to be forgotten or suppressed—and hence are probably historical in nucleus.

Nor were traditions of Aaron's dreadful exploits preserved to tarnish gratuitously his dignity and authority. The cultic aetiology of Aaron and the bull probably has its roots in Israelite traditions of Aaronic priests in Bethel who, in the ninth to eighth centuries B.C.E. after the united monarchy split in two, claimed Aaron as the creator of the iconography that adorned their temple—the young bull, which, from their point of view, was no less orthodox than the cherub iconography of Jerusalem, the capital of Judah. The expression "Behold your god(s) O Israel who brought you up from the land of Egypt" appears both in the account in Exodus 32 and in 1 Kings 12:28 when Jeroboam, king of the northern kingdom, set up his cultus in Dan and Bethel. The legend concerning Aaron was then turned backward into angry polemic by non-Aaronid priests—to be precise, by priests who traced their lineage to Moses and whose traditions are found in the Elohistic Epic source.

The conflict stories are inexplicable unless they arose in historical conflict and rivalry between a Moses group and an Aaron group, more precisely in the rivalry and conflict between Israel's two priestly houses, one the Zadokite family stemming from Aaron, the other a Mushite (Moses-ite) or Levitic family that claimed descent from Moses.

There is evidence of rivalry as late as the time of David when he chose two joint high priests for his national shrine and cultus—a remarkable phenomenon unless answering a political need in David's attempt to unify his realm and legitimize his new shrine in Jerusalem. The high priest Zadok can be traced to the Aaronids of Hebron, the site of an important ancient shrine in Judah; the high priest Abiathar, to the old Mushite priesthood of the shrine at Shiloh in the north. Eventually, the Levites of Mosaic descent lost their rights to be altar priests in Jerusalem and became a second-class, subservient clergy.

The evidence of the bitter conflict between the priestly houses survives in our biblical traditions. The priestly tradent, belonging to the Aaronids (i.e., Zadokites), when bringing into final form this mass of Tetrateuchal traditions, dared not suppress the stories of conflict, despite the fact that in his day the Aaronids were wholly dominant. The stories had already become part of a well known, authoritative Epic tradition.

Traditions about Reuben also yield evidence of Israel's early religious and social history. Reuben effectively disappeared from its tribal territory—and probably from any serious role in later Israelite history—in the course of the 11th century B.C.E.[21] The tribal allotment ceased to be called Reuben, and this area is usually referred to, as we have observed, as the plains or steppes of Moab. In the 11th-century Blessing of Moses (Deuteronomy 33) we find the plea: "Let Reuben live and not die, Although his men be few." Yet strangely, Reuben is called the firstborn of Jacob.

Genealogies in ancient Israel—and indeed, more widely, among tribal groups that create segmentary genealogies—always reflect some sociological and historical reality. The Chronicler reflects, if not bewilderment at Reuben's place in the genealogy, at least the clear judgment that Reuben was unworthy of the birthright, and that, in fact, it went to Joseph, though Judah became preeminent.[22] Chronicles notes, however, that one must write genealogies with Reuben as the firstborn. I contend that Reuben's place in the genealogy is evidence that Reuben once played a major role in Israelite society, even a dominant one, either political or religious or both.

So important was the role of Reuben that it could not be eradicated or forgotten. Pursuing this line leads to the conclusion that the cycle of traditions rooted in the plains of Moab, in ancient Reuben, in which Moses plays a dominant role, and in the related Midianite tradition, rests on historical memories, very early epic memories. This does not mean that the modern historian can treat these memories uncritically as history. Traditional memories may have distorted, telescoped or reshaped the core. This happens to orally transmitted narrative, even when it is preserved in the formulas and themes of oral poetry. But in pursuing his critical task, the modern historian can often ferret out important material for the history of Israelite religion and society.

WARRIOR GOD BAʿAL

Caption on page 34.

CHAPTER 2

THE DEVELOPMENT OF ISRAELITE RELIGION

HS: You spoke of using archaic poetry in the Bible to ferret out the history of Israelite religion and society. How do you tell what is archaic and old and what isn't?

FMC: One of the first two monographs that Noel Freedman and I wrote was on just this subject.[1] In the book, we attempted to isolate archaic poetry by using a series of typologies. Typological sequences are used to date scripts, pots, grammatical usage, prosodic canons and rhetorical devices, spelling practices, art forms and musical styles, architecture, dress fashions, armor and automobiles. The typologies we used in the analysis of archaic poetry included dating linguistic usage, vocabulary, morphology (notably of the verb system and pronominal elements and particles), syntax, spelling styles (a precarious task since spelling was usually revised over the centuries of scribal transmission), prosodic styles and canons, and finally mythological and religious traits.

Extrabiblical Canaanite and Hebrew inscriptions have provided the basis for a typological description of Hebrew poetry in the Bible, controlling the more subjective procedure of analyzing biblical literature and developing its typologies only on the basis of internal evidence. Poetry particularly lends itself to this procedure because its metrical structure and set formulas resist, in some measure, the pressures to modernize that shape less structured prose.

More subjective, but no less important, is the historical typology of ideas, particularly religious ideas. In archaic biblical poetry one finds survivals of raw mythology. In Psalm 29, a lightly revised Baʿal hymn, Yahweh is celebrated as the storm god whose voice is the thunder and whose bolts shatter the cedars of Lebanon. His roar "makes (Mount) Lebanon to dance like a young bull, (Mount) Sirion like a young buffalo" (Psalm 29:6). Archaic poetry delights in recounting the theophany (or visible manifestation) of the storm god as the Divine Warrior who marches out to war or who returns in victory to his temple (or mountain abode). In the oracles of rhapsodist prophets—such as Isaiah or Jeremiah—this language comes to be regarded as uncouth, if not dangerous, and is characteristically replaced in revelations by word, audition or vision of the heavenly council of Yahweh. Instead of thunder we get the word, the judgment.

HS: The still, small voice.

FMC: Just so. The still, small voice is a genuine oxymoron. The Hebrew should be translated "a silent sound." And the meaning is that Yahweh, whose theophanic appearance Elijah sought, passed with no perceptible noise.

HS: As opposed to passing in the storm.

STELE SHOWING WARRIOR GOD BAʿAL, page 32. On this stele from Ugarit, on the Mediterranean coast of modern Syria, the god Baʿal wields a club in his right hand and a lance with branches representing lightning in his left. This 14th- or 13th-century B.C.E. limestone slab measures nearly 18 inches high and 20 inches across. Many descriptions of God in the Hebrew Bible are as awe-inspiring as the image on this stele. "The voice of the Lord breaks the cedars, the voice of the Lord breaks the cedars of Lebanon," asserts the psalmist in Psalm 29. "He makes Mount Lebanon to dance like a young bull, Mount Sirion like a young buffalo."

Based on his studies of literary forms, Professor Cross believes that Psalm 29 is an early Hebrew poem, a lightly revised hymn to Baʿal, with mythological ideas embedded in it. The dominant image in this and other early Hebrew poems is a storm god who marches to war on behalf of his people and returns victorious to his temple or mountain abode. This image of God, Cross points out, was rejected by later prophets like Isaiah and Jeremiah in favor of a deity who reveals his intentions by word rather than deed.

Elijah Flees to Sinai (Horeb) and Yahweh Silently Appears (1 Kings 19:1-3,8-12)

[1]When Ahab told Jezebel all that Elijah had done and how he had put all the prophets of Ba'al to the sword, [2]Jezebel sent a messenger to Elijah, saying, "Thus and more may the gods do if by this time tomorrow I have not made you like one of them." [3]Frightened, Elijah fled at once for his life....

[8]Elijah walked forty days and forty nights as far as the mountain of God at Horeb. [9]There he went into a cave, and there he spent the night.

Then the word of the Lord came to him. He said to him, "Why are you here, Elijah?" [10]He replied, "I am moved by zeal for the Lord, the God of Hosts, for the Israelites have forsaken Your covenant, torn down Your altars, and put Your prophets to the sword. I alone am left, and they are out to take my life." [11]"Come out," He called, "and stand on the mountain before the Lord."

And lo, the Lord passed by. There was a great and mighty wind, splitting mountains and shattering rocks by the power of the Lord; but the Lord was not in the wind. After the wind—an earthquake; but the Lord was not in the earthquake. [12]After the earthquake—fire; but the Lord was not in the fire. And after the fire—a still, small voice.

FMC: Yes. Yahweh passed silently, but happily, engaged in conversation with Elijah. The account in 1 Kings 19 (see box, above) of Elijah's pilgrimage to Mount Sinai (to escape the wrath of Jezebel) is most interesting. It comes at the climax of a battle in which Yahwism seemed about to be overcome by Ba'alism, that is, by the sophisticated polytheism of the Phoenician court. Elijah goes to the mountain, to the very cave from which Moses glimpsed the back of Yahweh as he passed reciting his (Yahweh's) names.

Elijah is portrayed as a new Moses seeking a repetition of the old revelation to Moses on Sinai, but one marked by storm, earthquake and fire—in short, by the language of the storm theophany, the characteristic manifestation of Ba'al. In 1 Kings 19 there is wind and earthquake and fire, but the narrative, in vivid repeated phrases, tells us that Yahweh is not in the storm, Yahweh is not in the earthquake, Yahweh is not in the fire. He passes imperceptibly, and then speaks a word to Elijah, giving him a new vocation.

In the prophetic literature from the ninth century B.C.E. to the Babylonian Exile in the sixth century B.C.E., the language of revelation using the imagery of the storm is rare or missing. It does return in baroque form in what I call proto-Apocalyptic (I prefer that label to so-called Late Prophecy). See, for example, the vision of the storm chariot that introduces the Book of Ezekiel. The storm theophany is essentially the mode of revelation of Ba'al. By contrast the mode of revelation of 'El is the word, the decree of the Divine Council.[2]

In the virile, unchallenged vigor of early Yahwism, borrowing the language of the storm theophany was acceptable. In the era of the prophets, the language of 'El was deemed safer. I suspect that the ancient Israelites may have said simply—in our terms—that Yahweh decided to change his normative mode of self-disclosure.

HS: You have mentioned that there must have been some conflict in the course of the Israelite settlement in the hill country of Canaan. There is much talk these days about the historical reliability, or lack thereof, of the conquest stories such as the victories at Jericho and Ai. How do these fit into your theory?

FMC: In the case of Jericho and Ai (the name means the ruin), there was no occupation in the period of the conquest/settlement. There may have been some squatters at one or both sites, but the great, fortified cities did not exist, only their ruins. There are also problems in Transjordan. Heshbon, capital of one of the Amorite kingdoms destroyed by Israel (according to biblical tradition), seems to have been founded after the entry of Israel into their land. We generally date this entrance to the time of Ramesses II (1279-1212 B.C.E.) or the time of Merneptah (1212-1202 B.C.E.). New ceramic evidence for the date of collared-rim jars—a marker of the early Israelites—suggests a date no later than Ramesses II for the beginning of the settlement.[3]

HS: The Merneptah Stele dates to 1207 B.C.E.

FMC: Yes, to the fifth year of Merneptah.

HS: At that time, Israel was already in the land, settled, according to the Merneptah Stele. What do you do with that? In this stele, the most

powerful man in the world, the pharaoh, not only knows about this peo-
ple Israel in the land—this is not some commercial document concern-
ing some Israelite about whom we have no information, whether he is
a single individual or a member of a marginal tribe or whatever. This
people, Israel, has come to the attention of pharaoh himself. And pharaoh
claims that his victory over this people Israel in Canaan is one of the
most significant accomplishments in his reign.

FMC: I am not sure I would call Merneptah the most powerful man
in the world at this time. Surely Tukulti-Ninurta I of the Middle
Assyrian empire, the conqueror of Babylon, the first Assyrian king
to add the title "king of Babylon" to his titulary, has a better claim.
But never mind.

The Merneptah Stele is important, but it needs to be read with a
critical perspective.[4] Most of the stele contains hymns, or strophes
of a long hymn, about the defeat of various groups of Libyans. The
final hymn, or strophe, in which Israel is named, describes
Merneptah's conquests ranging from Hatti (the Hittite empire), Libya
and the Sea Peoples to Canaan. Then there are claims at the end of
the hymn "that every single land is pacified, everyone who roams
about is subdued," justifying John Wilson's remark that the text is
a "poetic eulogy of a universally victorious pharaoh." The stele is
written in parallelistic poetry. Israel is found in the quatrain:

> Ashkelon has been carried off;
> Gezer has been seized;
> Yanoʿam has been made into nothing,
> Israel is laid waste; his seed is not.

Around this quatrain, in an envelope or circle construction, are
the lines:

> Plundered is the [land] of Canaan...
> Palestine (Hurru) has become a widow for Egypt.

Interestingly, one name for Canaan is male; the other one (Hurru)
is female. This was no doubt a conscious device of the poet. Israel,
marked in Egyptian with the determinative sign for the name of a
people, not of a place or a state, is in parallel to Ashkelon and Gezer,
and more closely to Yanoʿam, all three of which are marked with the

determinative for city-states. This suggests the scale of importance given to Israel.

Further, the pharaoh Merneptah added to his official titulary the title "Seizer of Gezer," suggesting strongly that of the list of entities in Canaan, Gezer was preeminent. I would conclude that the Israel of the stele was a small people, perhaps villagers or pastoralists living in the central hill country, but not the full 12-tribe league of greater Canaan. The stele, moreover, says that he left Israel destroyed and without seed.

HS: Obviously that is wrong. But Israel must have been in the land. That's 1207, the end of the 13th century. That is before Iron I, is it not?

FMC: Yes to all points. The beginning of the Iron Age we label with a round number, 1200, but we might add plus or minus a decade or so. But to address your main point, when we say that Israel was in the land, what do we mean? Jacob/Israel is, of course, the eponymous ancestor chosen to head the genealogies of the tribes. But it is not obvious, or even credible to me, given the language of the stele, to suppose that the Israel of the stele is identical with the Israelite confederacy as it developed in the late 12th and 11th centuries. The proper name of the early league was actually the Kindred of Yahweh (ʿam yahweh). In my judgment, the first reference to the full confederacy is in the late 12th century (in the Song of Deborah, Judges 5).

MERNEPTAH STELE. "Israel is laid waste; his seed is not," Pharaoh Merneptah boasted on this stele dating to 1207 B.C.E., his fifth regnal year. "Plundered is the [land] of Canaan..." the stele says in the lines just preceding the mention of Israel. "Ashkelon has been carried off; Gezer has been seized; Yanoʿam has been made into nothing." The Canaanite campaign described here was waged at the beginning of Merneptah's rule, in 1212 B.C.E.

The reference to Israel—the earliest one outside the Bible—is slightly to the left of center in the second line from the bottom (see detail). Determinatives (unpronounced signs) attached to the place names indicate that Ashkelon, Gezer and Yanoʿam were cities and that Canaan was a foreign land; the determinative for Israel, however, indicates that the term referred to a people rather than a place. The Merneptah Stele shows that a people called Israel existed in 1212 B.C.E. and that the pharaoh of Egypt not only knew about them, but also felt it was worth boasting about having defeated them in battle.

Professor Cross believes that, at that time, Israel was still a small people, mostly pastoralists and villagers who inhabited the central hill country of Canaan. He believes they did not coalesce into the 12-tribe league known from the Bible until the 12th century B.C.E.

HS: What was the Israel mentioned in the Merneptah Stele?

FMC: I cannot answer satisfactorily—elements of later Israel.

HS: A particular tribe?

FMC: Perhaps a group of tribes or clans, perhaps—to speculate further—a group in the area of Shechem, about which we have very early cultic traditions going back into the 12th century.

HS: And they were somehow related to the people who later became the 12-tribe league?

FMC: I should think so. But I am not sure that this Israel and the Midianite-Moses group, which so strongly shaped early Israelite religion,[5] were united yet. At present, I do not think there is sufficient data to decide such questions.

HS: We don't really know that there was ever a 12-tribe league, do we?

FMC: I am among those who think there was a 12-tribe league. Twelve was a round number, and there is documentation of 12-tribe leagues both in Greece and in the south of Syria-Palestine. You could always arrange your tribes and clans so as to come out with 12.

HS: By jiggling the numbers?

FMC: Yes. Is Levi one of the 12? And what about the half-tribes of Manasseh and Ephraim (Joseph's sons), rather than Joseph? The number 12 also seems to have marked the leagues of Ishmael, Edom and Seir (Genesis 25:13-16, 36:10-19, 36:20-30, respectively).

HS: Would you agree with me if I suggest that the Merneptah Stele seems to indicate that there was an Israel in Canaan perhaps as early as 1250?

FMC: Pottery usually associated with the early elements of Israel perhaps begins as early as the second half of the 13th century. But the Merneptah Stele tells us only that by 1207, a group of people—

settled in villages or nomadic, but not constituting a state—called Israel was defeated.

HS: Are you sure enough of the dates that you can say that the villages that sprang up in the central hill country of Canaan didn't appear until after the Merneptah Stele?

FMC: One is never certain within a generation of pottery dates. There is now some evidence for collared-rim jars as early as the late 13th century. But most of the evidence for the foundation of these villages is Iron I, the early 12th century, at least in the view of ceramic specialists (of which I am not one). I have dated one inscription on a collared-rim jar to the late 13th century, but with the recent lowering of

INSCRIBED JAR HANDLE, from Raddana, about ten miles north of Jerusalem, bears (from top to bottom) the letters ʾalep (A), ḥet (Ḥ) and *lamed* (L). Adding the letter *dalet* (D) completes the name ʾAḥîlûd, a name known from contemporaneous references in 2 Samuel 8:16 and 20:24.

Professor Cross, applying his expertise in paleography (the study of script style and placement), dated this jar handle to about 1200 B.C.E. Cross believes the earliest Israelites may have been of patriarchal stock living in the Shechem area. They formed a covenant of clans early in the 12th century; this "proto-Israel" was later joined by followers of Moses, devotees of Yahweh who entered Canaan from the east.

the Egyptian chronology, my date too must be lowered, to about 1200 or the early 12th century. My dating of this inscription was based purely on paleographic grounds; at the time, I am embarrassed to say, I was innocent of the knowledge that the handle on which the inscription was scratched was from a collared-rim jar.[6]

HS: I see a problem here. The Merneptah Stele indicates the emergence of a people named Israel, which must have developed before Merneptah heard about them and was concerned about them and wanted to brag about defeating them. So I say that Israel was in the land sometime, conservatively, around 1230 B.C.E.

FMC: I cannot disprove that, but I can continue to ask what size the Israel of the stele was, and what its relation was to the later 12-tribe league.

HS: Then if you say that these villages in the hill country did not spring up until 1180 or so, there is a gap.

FMC: Not necessarily. I have said, basing my views on such studies as those of Stager and Finkelstein, that most of these villages appear to date from the beginning of the Iron Age. Some scenarios can be created to accommodate the data.

Let's say that in the Shechem area, home of ʿApiru, tribal elements of patriarchal stock consolidated themselves in a covenant of *ʾEl-berit* (ʾEl of the Covenant) (Judges 9:46; cf. Joshua 24 and the rites at Shechem). The covenanted clans may have been called by the patriarchal epithet Jacob/Israel. One patriarchal cultic aetiology has Jacob/Israel purchasing a plot in Shechem and setting up an altar "to ʾEl, the god of Israel [i.e., of Jacob]" (Genesis 33:20).

Traditions of the cult of Shechem recorded in the Bible, in which the law was recited and a ceremony of covenant renewal was held at intervals, must have been very early because Shechem was destroyed in the second half of the 12th century. Such an Israel may have had nothing to do with other groups of clans coming into the land from the east—e.g., the Moses group, devotees of Yahweh, the ʾEl of the south—until sometime later. This Moses group is described as entering Canaan from Reuben and moving into what would be called Judah, by way of Gilgal. Still other groups of tribes in the north, in Gilead and in the far south may have been added (through the mechanism of covenant-making) to the expanding confederation, making up, finally, the 12-tribe league of tradition.

How long such a process would have taken we do not know. How much conflict and warfare was involved as the league pushed out into the uninhabited portions of the central hill country we do not know. We know the expansion was completed by the time of Saul, and I think it highly likely that it was completed by the end of the 12th century. That is, a process that began slowly accelerated rapidly in the course of the 12th century. I am aware that in large part our reconstruction of this era is a skein of speculations. But at least our speculations try to comprehend all the bits of data we possess at the moment and to interpret them in a parsimonious way.

HS: Let's go back to Jericho and Ai. You said there were no cities there in the late 13th century, when we would suppose that the conquests had taken place? What do you make of these stories? Is there any history in the biblical stories?

FMC: The conquests of the walled city of Jericho and the great bastion of Ai were not the work of invading Israelites. These cities were destroyed earlier (and at different times). In the account of the fall of Jericho, moreover, there is a great deal of telltale folklore and literary ornamentation. The story of Rahab the harlot is a masterpiece of oral literature (Joshua 2).

HS: But it's also full of an enormous number of details that fit the location of Jericho, fit the environment, fit the time of year, fit the people— extraordinary details and even a destruction. The layperson says okay, maybe the Israelites attributed their victory to some kind of divine cause, but what is preserved here is a real victory that has been elaborated in an epic that attributes a divine cause to a victory that, in fact, has natural causes.

FMC: There are two issues here: (1) whether there is any historical reality lying behind the story of the conquest of Jericho, and (2) whether one can explain away divine causes as natural causes.

The latter does not really concern us here, though I have never understood why literalists and fundamentalists wish to explain away divine miracles by searching for natural or scientific explanations. To get rid of God in order to preserve the historicity of a folkloristic narrative strikes me as an instance of robbing Peter to pay Paul.

The first question is more serious. The details of local color were available to any singer of tales who had visited Jericho. Jericho had undergone a tremendous destruction of an earlier city and lay there in impressive ruins. I am inclined to think that a pre-Israelite epic tradition sang of the destruction, adding marvelous details over time, and that later Israelite singers, composing an epic of Israel's coming into the land, added the Jericho tale to the complex of oral narratives in their repertoire. Such expansions of epic narrative are characteristic of the process of the creation and transmission of epic and should not be the occasion of surprise.

HS: Where then do you see the conquest in the Israelite occupation of Canaan?

FMC: There was a great deal of disturbance in this period and the destruction of many sites. It is difficult in any single case to be sure who was the agent of destruction. Merneptah and the Sea Peoples were busy in the south and along the coast. Sites in the north like Hazor or Bethel are better candidates for Israelite conquest. But I am inclined to credit the consistent witness of early Hebrew poetry that Yahweh led Israel in holy wars and not attempt to trace the conquest in the archaeological record.

There are destructions enough to accommodate all parties. As I observed before, the 12-tribe league consolidated itself in the land with extreme rapidity. The speed of the formation of the league would, I think, require military conflict for success, and military conflict would in turn speed the formation of the league.

HS: We are talking about a couple of hundred years, are we not?

FMC: From Merneptah to the end of the 12th century is a century. By the time of the composition of early biblical poetry in the late 12th and 11th centuries B.C.E., these poets assume a more or less homogeneous religious group, a tribal system with a number of sodalities (brotherhoods or communities)—a league militia, a cultic establishment or religious society, priestly and lay leaders.

HS: Let's turn to the religion of Israel. You have stressed the continuities between Israelite religion and what went before, especially Canaanite and Amorite religion. You have emphasized the relationships and the development from earlier and contemporaneous West Semitic religions, isn't that correct?

FMC: I do underline continuities between West Semitic and Israelite religion. This is partly in reaction to the past generation that stressed the novelty and uniqueness of Israelite religion. Those claims have now been smothered by a cascade of new evidence, religious texts won by the archaeologist's spade.

My own philosophy of history maintains that there are no severely radical, or *sui generis*, innovations in human history. There must be continuity, or the novel will be unintelligible or unacceptable. This does not, however, mean that nothing new emerges. On the contrary, new elements do emerge, but in continuity with the past.

Let me illustrate with an example in paleography. All letters change over time, but the changes cannot be so radical as to be unrecognizable. If they are, the writing will be illegible. Change exhibits continuity, but genuinely new styles do emerge. A letter, let us say an ʾalep, can change from one shape to another over a long period of time, so that one would never recognize the late form as developed from the early. But if the whole typological series is laid out for scrutiny, the continuity from one form to another is continuous and wholly intelligible (see chart, p. 46).

One can speak of revolutions in history or revolutions in religious conceptions and insights. But these great changes are prepared for before they emerge. They may be precipitated swiftly, but if sufficient detail is known, one is able to perceive links and continuities. The new emergent takes up the past into itself.

HS: What is unique and distinct about Israelite religion, and how did it emerge?

FMC: Near Eastern religion, and especially West Semitic religion, has at its heart a cycle of myths about the establishment of kingship among the gods. The cosmogonies and rituals have two levels: (1) the celebration of the victory of the god of fertility and life and order over the unruly old powers of chaos and death, and (2) the establishment of the earthly kingdom after the heavenly model, a ritual attempt to bring the king, the nation and the people into harmony with the gods and the state into the eternal orders of creation. This is a profoundly static vision of ideal reality. Such religion is concerned with eternity, not with time or history.

At the heart of biblical religion, on the other hand, is not imitation of the gods but a celebration of historic events located in ordinary time, events that, in theory at least, can be dated, events in which historical figures like Moses play a central role. To be sure, in Israelite Epic the hero is a Divine Warrior, Yahweh, the god of armies. This is, if you wish, a mythological feature that illuminates history and gives it meaning, direction and a goal.

DEVELOPMENT OF ʾALEP. The chart shows the first letter of the alphabet, which became the Hebrew ʾalep, and how it changed over time. The earliest form (top left) is in the shape of an ox head, the word for which began with the sound of the letter. Moving to the right, the ʾalep evolves, although even the Greek alpha and Latin A as we know them preserve the earliest appearance.

Like the evolution of ʾalep, larger historical developments also demonstrate continuity amidst change. Professor Cross sees the development of ʾalep as an encapsulation of his concept of history. "My own philosophy of history," Cross says, "[is] that there are no severely radical innovations in human history. There must be continuity, or the novel will be unintelligible or unacceptable. New elements do emerge, but in continuity with the past."

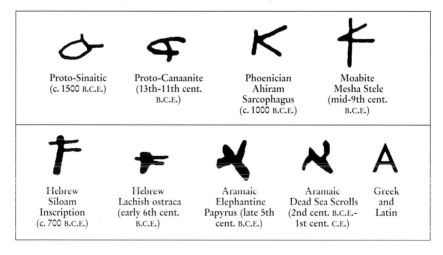

Proto-Sinaitic (c. 1500 B.C.E.)	Proto-Canaanite (13th-11th cent. B.C.E.)	Phoenician Ahiram Sarcophagus (c. 1000 B.C.E.)	Moabite Mesha Stele (mid-9th cent. B.C.E.)
Hebrew Siloam Inscription (c. 700 B.C.E.)	Hebrew Lachish ostraca (early 6th cent. B.C.E.)	Aramaic Elephantine Papyrus (late 5th cent. B.C.E.)	Aramaic Dead Sea Scrolls (2nd cent. B.C.E.-1st cent. C.E.)	Greek and Latin

Epic memory and hope gave identity to Israel. Israel's vocation—a nation of slaves, freed by a historical redemption—was to establish a community of justice. In the new Israel, the ethical was not defined by hierarchical structures in a society established in the created order; we do not find justice as equity according to class. Rather, justice is defined in egalitarian terms; it is redemptive, it frees slaves, uplifts the poor, gives justice to the widow and orphan, loves with an altruistic amity both one's neighbor (i.e., fellow member of the kinship community) and the resident alien or client ("sojourner" in the King James Version) *as oneself.*

The system of land tenure treats the land as a usufruct [something that can be used by all], a provisional loan from the Divine Landlord, and its largesse is to be distributed with a free hand to everyone in need. Rent and interest and the alienation of the land were prohibited—at least in the ideal law codes preserved by Deuteronomistic and Priestly circles in Israel.

The religious obligation laid on the Israelite is "to do justice and love mercy" (Micah 6:8) in the here and now, not to be preoccupied with ritual and sacrifice or intent on bargaining with the deity for an individual, eternal salvation. According to the prophetic teaching, Israel was to construct a community of social responsibility, of justice, of compassion and of brotherhood.

This understanding of the business of religion—at least in emphasis—contrasts with religions that sanctify an order of divine and human kingship. In one sense, Israel's emergent faith seeks the secularization of religion. For the prophet, neither the person of the king, nor the Temple in Jerusalem, nor any other institution of society is divine or sacral in more than a provisional way, and the survival of these institutions depends on their fulfillment of the command to "Let justice well up as waters,/ Righteousness as a mighty stream" (Amos 5:24).

Israel's religion is historical. It offers no escape from history, but rather plunges the community into the midst of historic time.

HS: *You don't mention ethical monotheism.*

FMC: I have been talking about the ethical, and about history as the realm of the ethical. What interests me is Israel's peculiar understanding

Yahweh Decrees Death to Other Gods (Psalm 82)

*¹God stands in the divine
    assembly;
among the divine beings He
    pronounces judgment.
²How long will you judge
    perversely,
showing favor to the wicked?
³Judge the wretched and the
    orphan,
vindicate the lowly and the poor,
⁴rescue the wretched and the
    needy;
save them from the hand of the
    wicked.*

*⁵They neither know nor
    understand,
they go about in darkness;
all the foundations of the earth
    totter.
⁶I had taken you for divine
    beings,
sons of the Most High, all of
    you;
⁷but you shall die as men do,
fall like any prince.
⁸Arise, O God, judge the earth,
for all the nations are Your
    possession.*

of the ethical. Monotheism also emerged in Israel, of course, as it did elsewhere. Once again, I am more interested in the specific type of monotheism found in the Bible than in monotheism as an abstract category.

If we define monotheism as a theoretical or philosophic affirmation that "no more than one god exists," we have not recognized, I think, what is most important about Israel's concept of their deity. Why is one god better than two or none? The biblical view of God is not abstract or ontological; it is existential. What is important is the relation of the worshiper and the community to God—obedience to and love of God, rather than affirmation of his sole existence.

The *Shema* (found in Deuteronomy 6) is often misunderstood as an abstract affirmation of the existence of one God. It is usually translated: "Hear O Israel: the Lord is our God, the Lord is one." Literally translated, it reads, "Hear O Israel: Yahweh is our God, Yahweh alone." The substitution of "the Lord" for the personal name of the Israelite God (Yahweh) confuses matters. To translate "the Lord is one" makes sense as an affirmation of a monotheistic faith. But to translate literally "Yahweh is one" makes no sense. Who would claim that more than one Yahweh existed?

Israel was required to worship only one God and to confess his unique and universal power in the historical realm. At least in early

Israel, Israelite religion did not systematically deny the existence of other gods or divine powers. In Psalm 82, Yahweh stands up in the council of the gods and decrees the death of the gods because of their failure to judge their peoples justly, and then Yahweh takes over. One can argue that the psalm at once admits to the existence of other gods and asserts that Yahweh killed them off—instant monotheism. I prefer to speak of existential monotheism in defining Israel's credo.

HS: What you are describing may be henotheism.

FMC: Well, henotheism historically has been used to refer to the belief in one local god who enjoys domination over his local turf—Israel or Moab or Ammon. One god per country, so to speak. I don't think that Israel ever had such a belief, and indeed, even in pre-Israelite Canaanite mythology, the great gods were universal. The myths speak of the land or mount of heritage of some of the gods, but these are favorite abodes, and the expressions indicate no limits on their power or, normally, their ability to travel over the cosmos.[7]

Monolatry is another term that many scholars use—the *worship* of only one god. This term, also, I regard as too restrictive in defining Israelite faith and practice. In Israel, Yahweh was creator and judge in the divine court. Other divine beings existed, but they were not important; they exercised little authority or initiative. If they retained a modicum of power, let's say to heal or provide omens, the Israelite was forbidden to make use of their power.

Quite early, magic was proscribed. The existence and effectiveness of magic was not denied or theoretically repudiated, but an Israelite was not to touch it. Indeed, there is a law requiring that a sorceress or witch be put to death (Exodus 22:18). Nor is the transcendent one, the God of Israel, to be manipulated.

In short, Israel defined its God and its relation to that God in existential, relational terms. They did not, until quite late, approach the question of one God in an abstract, philosophical way. If I had to choose between the two ways of approaching the deity, I should prefer the existential, relational way to the abstract, philosophical way. I think it is truer—or, in any case, less misleading—to say that God is an old Jew with a white beard whom I love than to say that God is the ground of being and meaning, or to say that God is a name

A Myth Resurfaces—Yahweh Overcomes the Sea
(Isaiah 51:9-11)

⁹*Awake, awake, clothe yourself
  with splendor.
O arm of the Lord!
Awake as in days of old,
As in former ages!
It was you that hacked Rahab in
  pieces,
That pierced the Dragon.*
¹⁰*It was you that dried up the Sea,*

*The waters of the great deep;
That made the abysses of the Sea
A road the redeemed might walk.*
¹¹*So let the ransomed of the Lord
  return,
And come with shouting to Zion,
Crowned with joy everlasting.
Let them attain joy and gladness,
While sorrow and sighing flee.*

denoting the ultimate mystery. I prefer the bold, primitive colors of the biblical way of describing God.[8]

HS: You have said that "in Israel, myth and history always stood in strong tension, myth serving primarily to give a cosmic dimension, a transcendent meaning to the historical, rarely functioning to dissolve history."

FMC: I don't remember that precise quotation but it sounds like me. Let me quote a better statement from the preface to *Canaanite Myth and Hebrew Epic*:

> Characteristic of the religion of Israel is a perennial and un-relaxed tension between the mythic and the historical....Israel's religion emerged from a mythopoeic past under the impact of certain historical experiences which stimulated the creation of an epic cycle and its associated covenant rites of the early time. Thus epic, rather than the Canaanite cosmogonic myth, was featured in the ritual drama of the old Israelite cultus. At the same time the epic events and their interpretation were shaped strongly by inherited mythic patterns and language, so that they gained a vertical dimension in addition to their horizontal, historical stance. In this tension between mythic and historical elements the meaning of Israel's history became transparent.[9]

Let me illustrate with something concrete—the Song of the Sea in Exodus 15. This poem recounts a divine victory at the sea. Then the Divine Warrior marches with his chosen people to his mount of inheritance and builds his sanctuary, where he is revealed as king. The poem ends with the shout, "Let Yahweh reign, Forever and ever." This sequence of themes is really, in outline, the story of Baʿal's war with Sea (Yamm): Baʿal defeats Sea, builds his temple as a manifestation of the kingship won in his victory and is declared eternal king.

But there are, of course, differences in the biblical poem. Yahweh does not defeat the sea but creates a storm to drown the Egyptians. The sea is his tool, not his enemy, and his real foes are pharaoh and his chariots—human, historical foes. One is moved to ask, however,

SUMERIAN GOD NINURTA ATTACKING DRAGON. On a Sumerian shell inlay dating to about 2600 B.C.E., Ninurta attacks a fearsome seven-headed dragon. This mythical creature may have inspired the biblical Leviathan, which is sometimes said to have seven heads. In the popular imagination, taming Leviathan was one of God's feats during Creation. Psalm 74:13-14 exults, "Thou didst divide the sea by thy might;/ thou didst break the heads of the dragons on the waters./ Thou didst crush the heads of Leviathan,/ thou didst give him as food for the creatures of the wilderness."

God's mastery over the sea, during Creation and in the crossing of the Red Sea, was an important component of Israelite religion. Professor Cross points out similarities with the story of Baʿal, whose worshipers believed he vanquished Yamm, the god of the sea, before marching with his people to his mountain sanctuary to build his temple.

why the central, defining victory of the deity must take place at the sea. Why not the victory of the conquest? Why isn't the gift the Land of Promise, which is the climax of the old epic narrative?

Surely it is because the old mythic pattern survives and exercises influence. In Isaiah 51:9-11, the old myth resurfaces, so to speak, in the identification of the victory of Yahweh (or rather Yahweh's arm, symbol of his strength) in the battle of creation against the sea monster, and at the same time (time becoming fluid in mythic fashion) in the cleaving of a path through the sea for Israel to cross over, and (time again becoming fluid) with the eschatological new way through the desert built for the redeemed of the exile to march to Zion. The mythic garb in which historical events are dressed points to the transcendent meaning of the event at the sea and the march to the land. They are the familiar *magnalia dei* (wonders of God), the plot of the Israelite epic in new form.

HS: Are they historical in any sense that we understand that term, or do we have to do with a transformation of myth into mythical history?

FMC: Both. Many scholars are inclined to call much of biblical narrative mythology. I think this is misleading. On the other hand, I hesitate to use the term history. History in the modern context means a description and interpretation of human events arrived at by a specific scientific method. Among the stipulations of this method is agreement to eschew discussion of ultimate causation or meaning, those tasks supposedly being left to the philosopher of history or the theologian or the Marxist. You don't speak of divine acts or victories in writing history.

At best, the historian can describe people's beliefs about such matters. Attribution of events to miracle is disallowed on methodological grounds (not necessarily on philosophic or theological grounds, though frequently the postulates of the method become a negative metaphysics for the practitioner).

In short, the historian *qua* historian must put distance between himself and religious affirmations of Yahweh's divine direction of history. So to use the term historical is misleading in describing the constitutive genre of biblical narrative. Sometimes I use the term historic (*geschichtlich*) rather than history (*Historie*). I prefer to use the term epic; this term takes up into itself both the historic and mythic elements in the Hebrew Epic.

HS: *Is there a factual core?*

FMC: In the case of biblical epic and Greek heroic epic, yes. Included in the epic genre are narrative poems with differing amounts of factual, historical memories. Biblical epic, in my view, is on the more rather than the less side of the spread of historical elements.

HS: *Does the historical side matter?*

FMC: Yes. Without a historical core I doubt that the historic nature of Israelite religion with its particular values and ethics would have emerged from the Canaanite environment or, later, would have overcome its mythological rivals and survived to become a foundation of Western culture. Unless we are legitimately able to affirm the essential historical character of biblical religion, our religious tradition will tend to dissolve into ahistorical forms of religion—Docetism, Gnosticism, otherworldliness and kindred heresies.

This, of course, cannot be the reason we insist on a core of history underlying biblical narrative. Our claims must rest on objective historical analysis. But the issue has important consequences for Christianity and Judaism, and for the Western tradition, especially in a day in which diverse mystical and ahistorical religious lore is in vogue under the misleading label of multiculturalism.

The world of epic, in which there is a mixture of myth and history, is not distant from our experience. An American today often perceives his or her place in history in epic categories. There is our familiar Pilgrim epic. We, mostly of lowly birth and status, were freed from the persecution and chains of the Old World and led through the perils of the great ocean to a new land, a land flowing with milk and honey. (Mark Twain, standing on the shore of the Sea of Galilee, was unimpressed and exclaimed that the Lord would never have chosen the land of Canaan as the Holy Land if he had ever seen Lake Tahoe.)

The Mayflower covenant or pact was sealed by a company conscious of repeating the Israelite liberation and the covenant at Sinai, and members of the company sang psalms as the new land came into sight.

Two epic traditions have been said to mark much of better American fiction. There is a dark thread that presents the American experience in terms of a broken covenant. It is expressed variously. We are pictured as fouling and corrupting the pristine Land of Promise. You see this vividly in Faulkner's novels and in *Moby Dick*, one of the monuments of American literature, a novel full of biblical symbolism. These writers and others express guilt for the American story in our new land—the slaughter of the aborigines, the establishment of slavery, reversion to the class system, reversion to the greed and nationalism of the Old World from which we fled, crimes we swore to eradicate.

There is another thread—ebullient, optimistic, a plot taken from the normative American cowboy story or its ancestor, Cooper's *Leatherstocking Tales*. Americans are the good guys who, therefore, can shoot straighter, redeem the wilderness, create unlimited wealth, outrun, outwit and outdo lesser breeds. This epic thread is visible in absurd simplicity in the credo of Ronald Reagan—this is God's land; we are a city on a hill; Americans are God's people; the future belongs to us. Only the evil empire hinders our apotheosis.

We know that this epic, which informs our lives, is a mixture of myth and history. Few of us are descendants of the Pilgrims who came early to the new land. But in becoming part of the American community and its self-understanding, we live and relive the experience of the founding fathers, just as I think many (or most) Israelites who came late into the Land of Promise and who never saw Egypt did. In their festivals—and in ours—we regard ourselves as having been freed from the house of bondage and led to the Promised Land.

HS: Even today, in the Passover seder, Jews say that they were personally freed from Egypt.

FMC: Yes. Our history with its trappings of myth gives meaning to past and future. We live in a community of epic memories and expectation. I think that is the way human beings are meant to live and think—which reflects the influence on me of biblical religion.

HIEROGLYPHIC WRITING

Caption on page 58.

CHAPTER 3

HOW THE ALPHABET DEMOCRATIZED CIVILIZATION

HS: One of humankind's greatest achievements, if not the greatest, is the invention of the alphabet. It was invented only once. All alphabets ultimately derive from the original Semitic alphabet. It's astonishing to me that the invention came from this little point of a place on the globe, this tiny nothing of a place. If Cecil B. DeMille were doing this, he might say, "The Semites who brought you God now bring you the alphabet."

FMC: [Laughter]

HS: When was the alphabet invented?

FMC: We don't know precisely when or where. We have alphabetic inscriptions going back to the 16th, some say the 17th, century B.C.E. My guess is that the alphabet was invented in the 18th century, in the era when the West Semitic Hyksos ruled the Egyptian delta, and kindred folk ruled city-states in much of Syria-Palestine.[1] We can't be more specific, I think, than to locate the invention in Greater Canaan. However, it is not impossible that it was devised in Amorite or Canaanite chancelleries in the Egyptian delta.

HS: The earliest examples we have are from Canaan, aren't they?

FMC: Yes. Indeed, the earliest are from Palestine. For a long while, it was thought that the earliest Old Canaanite inscriptions in alphabetic pictographs were from Sinai, the so-called proto-Sinaitic inscriptions. They were generally dated incorrectly to the 18th century.[2]

HS: I thought (Sir Flinders) Petrie called it pretty close when he dated them to about 1500 B.C.E.[3]

FMC: That's right. Despite Petrie's sound arguments, the earlier date of (Sir Alan) Gardiner prevailed until William Foxwell Albright went to Serābîṭ el-Khâdem (in southwestern Sinai, where Petrie found his texts) and reestablished the 1500 B.C.E. date, a date subsequently confirmed by Israeli archaeologists.[4]

The Palestinian inscriptions in Old Canaanite (as we now call the early alphabetic pictographs) are in some cases earlier than the Sinaitic group, going back to the 16th century and possibly earlier.[5] They are not very impressive in size or number, but they do indicate that the script was in use generally in Canaan. By 1500 B.C.E. and a bit later, we have examples of most of the pictographic signs making up the alphabet.

A turning point comes in the 11th century. Inscribed arrowheads from the 11th century provide a missing link—now filled in—between

HIEROGLYPHIC WRITING, page 56. Before the invention of the alphabet, the two dominant writing systems in the Near East were Egyptian hieroglyphics and Mesopotamian cuneiform script. Both originated in picture writing, small drawings that initially represented objects—for example, the head of an ox for cattle. Gradually, the pictures became increasingly stylized until, in the case of cuneiform, they bore little or no resemblance to the objects they once depicted.

Hieroglyphs were of four kinds. Some represented objects or words; a second type represented syllables with several consonants; a third type represented single consonants—what we would colloquially call letters (but it never occurred to conservative Egyptian scribes to use these single-consonant signs as an alphabet); a fourth type of sign, called determinatives (a type shared with cuneiform), had no phonetic value but was used to classify accompanying words (for example, a name was classified as the name of a city or a people, depending on the determinative).

The example of hieroglyphic writing on page 56 is the bottom portion of a wooden stele (standing monument) from the tenth to eighth centuries B.C.E. The stele is divided in half vertically; at top, far left and far right, a priest named Harsiese, looking in two directions, makes offerings to the gods Rehorakhty and Atum, respectively. Interestingly, the text below the scene is written in different directions, each half following the direction of Harsiese's gaze above. The texts contain brief genealogies of Harsiese and praise for the gods.

the pictographic Old Canaanite script and the evolved linear script we call Early Phoenician linear. It is the Early Phoenician linear that is the immediate ancestor of Old Hebrew, Old Aramaic and indeed of the early Greek alphabet.

The finds of inscribed arrowheads plus finds at Ugarit, including abecedaries and a tablet transcribing into syllabic cuneiform the first syllable of the names of the Canaanite alphabetic signs [letters], have cleared away many disputed issues or unsolved problems in the early history of the alphabet.

HS: *What are these disputed issues or doubtful matters?*

FMC: Many have doubted that the invention of the alphabet was based on the acrophonic principle; that is, that each sign was a pictograph representing an object, the name of which began with the letter the sign was meant to represent.

HS: *What is the acrophonic principle? It really explains the invention of the alphabet, doesn't it?*

SUMERIAN PICTURE WRITING. Ancient people first used pictures to convey ideas and messages. The black stone tablet shown here dates to 3000 B.C.E. and records a land sale in ancient Sumer. Picture writing like this has a striking immediacy but is too cumbersome to be practical as a writing system.

FMC: Yes. If we illustrate the principle with English, then, let us say, *a* is for apple, *b* is for ball, *c* is for cat. If you pen the pictures cat-apple-ball, you have spelled out the word cab.

HS: In other words, you draw an apple and that becomes a*?*

FMC: Precisely. If you go to the Old Canaanite alphabet, the letter we call *a*, ʾalep in Hebrew, is the picture of a bull.

HS: A bull or an ox?

FMC: Ox usually means a castrated animal, at least in American English. The pictograph in question represents an ordinary bovine, presumably a bull.

RECTANGULAR CUNEIFORM TABLET. This cuneiform tablet is one of 16,500 found within a vast archive at Ebla, in modern Syria. The Ebla repository contained both round and rectangular tablets. Round tablets were usually smaller and were used for ephemeral records; rectangular tablets like this one were used to record royal letters, scribal textbooks, treaties and mythic tales. Cuneiform signs represented syllables and words but (except for Ugaritic) not what we would consider letters.

HS: The letter is just the head of the animal?

FMC: Yes. Actually, the singular ʾ*alep* is not used in Hebrew, only the plural meaning cattle. In older Semitic the word is used for both bull and ox.

   Bet means house; so you draw a little square with a door, and you have a house, which has the alphabetic value *b*. In this fashion you proceed through the alphabet. The letter *m*, *mem* in Phoenician from which the Hebrew alphabet is borrowed, *mayim* in Hebrew, means water; you represent the *m*-sound by a little squiggled line that looks like wavy water.

   Slowly such pictographs evolve into highly conventionalized linear signs that, at best, reveal only dimly the earlier pictograph. For example, *šin* was originally represented by the picture of a composite bow. Then it slowly changed into a simple zigzag line, Greek *sigma*. The letter ʿ*ayin*, which became *o* in Greek and English, was originally the picture of an eye with a pupil in it; ʿ*ayin* means eye. It then simplifies first to a round circle with a dot in the center, and then to an even simpler circle.

HS: The alphabet originated under the influence of Egyptian hieroglyphs, didn't it?

FMC: Egyptian hieroglyphic script was a primary influence.

HS: Can you explain that?

FMC: The Canaanite alphabet arose in an area where two important writing systems overlapped—Mesopotamian cuneiform, with its elaborate syllabary, and Egyptian writing, with its complex set of pictographs.

HS: Hieroglyphics?

FMC: Yes. The Canaanites, therefore, knew that there were alternate means of writing, more than one system. Indeed they used Akkadian cuneiform in the city-states of Canaan to write to their Egyptian overlords.[6] And West Semites, especially those in the

How Egyptian Hieroglyphs Became Semitic Letters

Egyptian symbol	Meaning	Egyptian word	Semitic letter	Meaning	Semitic word	Sound in Semitic
	home	pr		home	bet (*bayit* in Hebrew	b
	throw stick	ʿmˁt		throw stick	gaml (*gimel* in Hebrew)	g
	arm and hand	ʿ (a laryngeal sound not found in English		arm and hand	yod (*yad* in Hebrew)	y
	water	nt		water	mem (*mayim* in Hebrew)	m
	composite bow	iwnt		composite bow	than/thin (*shin* in Hebrew)	th

FROM HIEROGLYPHICS TO SEMITIC ALPHABET. This chart shows several symbols in Egyptian hieroglyphics (left) and in the early Semitic alphabet (center). Over time these symbols became transmuted into the letters *b*, *g*, *y*, *m* and *s* of our alphabet. The Semitic signs are barley distinguishable from their Egyptian predecessors, but their function is radically different. Each Semitic symbol represents the first sound in the name of the object depicted. A relatively small number of these signs could be juxtaposed to make a limitless number of words—the world's first alphabet.

ACROPHONIC PRINCIPLE. The drawing illustrates the acrophonic principle, in which symbols no longer stand for the objects they depict but for the first sound in the name of the object. In this example, the picture of the cat stands for the hard "c" sound, the apple adds the sound of "a," and the ball contributes the "b" sound; the pictures cat-apple-ball together spell "cab." Using the alphabet, which was originally developed on the basis of the acrophonic principle, all words could be "written" using fewer than 30 signs, an enormous simplification over earlier writing systems like hieroglyphics and cuneiform.

Canaanite port towns and the Nile delta, had commonly seen hieroglyphic monuments. So, when you think about it, it isn't surprising that it was in the Canaanite realm that the alphabet was invented.

A Canaanite scribe who was bilingual or trilingual, who could write in more than one writing system, evidently was freer to let his imagination range, to contemplate the possibility of other, simpler alternatives to the writing systems he knew. I think of the analogy of number systems. I was in graduate school before I discovered base-12 numbers (studying cuneiform); I had supposed that the decimal system, base-10 numbers, was part of the created order of the cosmos. And now, 40 years later, every grammar school child knows about computers and base-2 numbers.

In Egyptian writing, there are signs representing two-consonant combinations or three-consonant combinations. There are even signs for one consonant (plus any vowel—vowels were not ordinarily denoted in the hieroglyphic system). However, it never occurred to conservative Egyptian scribes that they could take these one-consonant signs and use them as an alphabet. This "pseudo-alphabet" existed unrecognized in their massive syllabary of 300 or 400 signs in regular use. Apparently its potential went unrecognized.

HS: In other words, they had letters, but they didn't know how to use them as an alphabet.

FMC: Yes. Scribal convention—spelling rules—required that they use the whole syllabary. A less conventional, and probably less well trained, Canaanite got the notion—why don't we simplify this grotesque system? Why not let one sign equal one consonant? In this way 27 or 28 signs became the basis for the alphabet.

Canaanite and West Semitic dialects have only three vowel areas, and each syllable begins with a consonant. This means that a writing system in which only consonants were denoted was practical and relatively unambiguous. Greeks, who use a language with a different vocalic system and vowels to initiate words and syllables, were forced early on to invent vowel letters—most taken from Phoenician consonants with no Greek equivalents.

There were two aspects to the invention. One was radical simplification. The second was the borrowing of many Egyptian hieroglyphic signs to use as the pictographs of the Canaanite alphabet. The pictographs were not given Egyptian values, however, but were assigned the names of the objects pictured in the Canaanite language.

For example, take the hieroglyphic sign for water. "Water" is *nt* in Egyptian. In the Canaanite pictographic script, this sign borrowed from hieroglyphic has the value *m* not *n*, because the word for water in Canaanite is *mem*; therefore the sign represents the letter *mem* or *m*. The same thing for other signs—house, hand, composite bow, eye and so on through the alphabet. A few signs were evidently invented when Egyptian did not provide the desired pictograph.

HS: You talked about two streams that influenced the invention of the alphabet. One was Egyptian hieroglyphics. What was the other stream?

FMC: I spoke of simplification and borrowing pictographs as two aspects of the invention. I have mentioned also the importance of the use of the cuneiform script, the primary script used in international correspondence. But the cuneiform syllabary did not contribute directly to the invention of the alphabet.

HS: It was a dead end, wasn't it?

FMC: Yes, it finally became moribund and disappeared. Actually, at one time the Canaanite alphabet was modified to be written with cuneiform wedges. At Ugarit a large number of tablets from the 14th century B.C.E., written in a Canaanite cuneiform alphabet, has been found, and this cuneiform system also has been found sporadically in Palestine and even in Cyprus.

HS: But that was simply an arbitrary invention based on the Semitic alphabet.

FMC: Yes. It was based on the alphabet but used the writing technique (cuneiform) originating in Mesopotamia. Oddly, but happily, the Ugaritic tablets are preserved in great numbers, so that we have more literature from high antiquity preserved on clay in the Canaanite cuneiform alphabet than we do in the pictographic and Early Phoenician linear alphabets. Inscriptions in Old Canaanite are rare.

The first "burst" of preserved texts is the corpus of inscribed arrowheads of the 11th century B.C.E. The fad of inscribing bronze arrowheads lasted for a brief century. In 1953 only one was known, the so-called Ruweiseh arrowhead, and it was misdated and misread. Then in 1954, J. T. Milik and I found three more. Now more than 25 or so are known (see photo, p. 66).

HS: Where did you find them?

FMC: In Jerusalem, in the *suq* [market] of the Old City, in the hands of antiquities dealers. We learned from extensive inquiries where they were found—in ʾEl-Khaḍr, a village near Bethlehem. Actually they were turned up in a field that was being plowed—a cache of many arrowheads, of which we acquired three, were inscribed with the same inscription: "Arrowhead of ʿAbd-labīʾt." The name ʿAbd-labīʾt, "Servant of the Lion-lady," appears also in a 14th-century list of archers from Ugarit.

The ʾEl-Khaḍr inscriptions are from the beginning of the 11th century B.C.E. Then, 25 years later, I came upon more of the ʾEl-Khaḍr hoard. I was reading some inscriptions on Samaritan coins in the elegant home of a Jerusalem lawyer when I noticed an arrowhead in a cabinet on the wall, and on closer look, I recognized the style of the ʾEl-Khaḍr pieces, which was confirmed when the inscription on the arrowhead mentioned the same ʿAbd-labīʾt. My lawyer friend informed me further that he knew of a similar piece in the hands of a private collector. So in 1980 I published the two new arrowheads, making five inscribed pieces in all from ʾEl-Khaḍr.

Most recently the Israel Museum acquired two arrowheads which have been entrusted to me for publication; and now there is a spectacular inscribed arrowhead in Elie Borowski's new Bible Lands Museum, which I have just published.[7] Most of these arrowheads appear to have belonged to high-ranking military officers.

One of the Israel Museum arrowheads is inscribed with a name and the title "captain of a thousand [*śrʾlp*]," or better, "brigadier." They are not *hoi polloi*. The title on the Bible Lands Museum arrowhead is *ʾiš šapaṭ*, "man," or better "retainer," of Šapaṭ. Remember the *anšê dawīd* the "retainers" or "heroes" of David (for example, 1 Samuel 23:3). The owner of the Bible Lands Museum arrowhead had a similar title and no doubt served a similar function.

INSCRIBED ARROWHEADS. Thanks to a fad—carving inscriptions on arrowheads—that flourished in the 11th century B.C.E., we now have a transitional link from proto-Canaanite script to the Early Phoenician linear script, the immediate ancestor of Old Hebrew, Old Aramaic and the early Greek alphabet. Three arrowheads in the original hoard found at ʾEl-Khadr in the 1950s were inscribed with the phrase "Arrowhead of ʿAbd-labiʾt," which means "Servant of the Lion-lady." ʿAbd-labiʾt also appears on a 14th-century B.C.E. list of archers from Ugarit, on the Mediterranean coast of modern Syria.

Some 25 years later, Professor Cross saw an arrowhead similar to the ʾEl-Khadr pieces that bore the name ʿAbd-labiʾt. Cross was told about another inscribed arrowhead owned by a private collector; thus, the number was raised to five. Recently three more have turned up.

The inscription on the obverse of the largest one (5 inches long) (top photo and drawing) reads "Arrowhead of Šemidaʿ son of Yiššabaʿ." The inscription on the reverse (bottom drawing and photo) reads "man [retainer] of Šapaṭ, Tyrian." The name Šapaṭ is also the name of the father of the biblical Elisha and a herdsman of David, among others. The title "man [retainer] of Šapaṭ" recalls ʾanšê Dawīd, "retainers of David" or "heroes of David" from 1 Samuel 23:3 and several other biblical passages. The inscription indicates that the owner of the arrowhead was a high-ranking military officer.

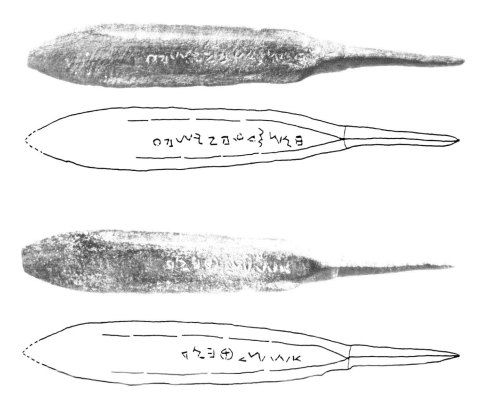

HS: Perhaps you would comment on the significance of the discovery of the alphabet.

FMC: Writing removes literature from dependence on fragile human memory. It makes thought visible and preserves it so it can be examined and reexamined at leisure. It records agreements and contracts permanently.

In the elaborate writing systems in use in Mesopotamia and in Egypt—cuneiform and hieroglyphics—reading and writing was the preserve of scholars. Writing remained, in effect, the exclusive preserve of the crown and the temple. The invention of the alphabet, with its great simplicity, broke this monopoly in principle.

Writing was not beyond the powers of ordinary people; with the use of the alphabet, literacy began to spread. Early alphabetic writing was completely phonetic; one had only to learn 22 characters (after 1200 B.C.E.), and to distinguish the significant consonantal sounds (phonemes) of one's own language.

HS: Elsewhere you have called this the democratization of culture. What do you mean by that?

FMC: Learning and culture need no longer be in the control of a very tiny elite, as in Mesopotamia where a great king brags that he can read a bit of cuneiform—a remarkable feat in his eyes. Religious lore—myth, ritual, magic, medicine—need no longer be the exclusive property of hierophants who manipulate gods and men.

Alphabetic writing spread quickly—I have said it spread like wildfire. When asked what I mean by quickly, I have replied that it took a millennium to become widespread and break the yoke of syllabic systems. But in terms of ancient history, this qualifies as swiftly. Meanwhile oral transmission, especially of literature and religious lore, persisted alongside writing. Gradually, however, oral transmission wanes and written transmission waxes—and we move into a new cultural realm.

If writing freezes thought and makes it visible, simple alphabetic writing makes thought and cultural lore easily and quickly visible and subject, with much greater ease, to analysis, criticism and logical perusal. Moreover, it makes the elements of culture much more widely available to all kinds of people and classes of society.

Logic and skepticism flourish only after alphabetic writing makes possible the examination and reexamination of an easily visualized record of a legal argument, a classification of scientific items, a philosophical discourse, a historical narrative or a piece of royal propaganda. It has been argued that the emergence of Greek logic awaited the development of the alphabet.

Two critical cultures developed in the vast sweep of ancient Near Eastern and Mediterranean history. One was Greece, with its alphabetic culture, its philosophy and skepticism. The second was Israel, with its rejection of the sacral claims of state and church and with its sustained prophetic critique of the mighty and wealthy—including priest and king—who oppressed the poor and the weak. Israel's attitudes towards its rulers, and the unjust society they created, are unique in the ancient Near East, where deified kings and hierarchical class structure were assumed to be part of the order of creation. Writing, alphabetic writing, I would suggest, made an important contribution to the development of what has been called the prophetic principle.

HS: There is a tremendous dispute among scholars as to when the Greeks adopted the Semitic alphabet, isn't there?

FMC: I belong steadfastly to the school of paleographers who believe that the borrowing was relatively early, in the second half of the 11th century B.C.E. Until the mid-11th century, the time of the transition from Old Canaanite to the linear Phoenician script, writing was multidirectional. Then in the late 11th century it shifted, permanently and exclusively, to right-to-left horizontal writing.

The Greeks borrowed the alphabet at a time when one could still write right to left, left to right, or boustrophedon ("as the ox ploughs," that is, in both directions), or in vertical columns. In each case, the stance of the signs faced away from the direction of writing. This created a tendency for stances to rotate over a given period of time. Multidirectional writing was borrowed by the Greeks with the alphabet. We know this from early Greek inscriptions. When the direction of Greek writing was stabilized, it was from left to right, contrary to Phoenician, which is right to left.

The shapes of the letters too, and their stances, tell us when the borrowing took place. The Greek letters show themselves to be derived from Phoenician letters of the second half of the 11th century. The most archaic Greek alphabets typologically—the scripts of the Cyclades and Crete—stand in elegant continuity with the scripts of the new, expanded corpus of 11th-century inscriptions on the inscribed arrowheads.

The continued insistence of many classicists on a much later date for the borrowing of the alphabet ultimately stems from the anti-Phoenician (if not anti-Semitic) impulse of an earlier generation of classical scholars. Often an older generation is followed by younger scholars with no awareness of this anti-Semitic bias. Also our expanded knowledge of the early history of the Old Canaanite and Phoenician scripts has not yet seeped into the classical discussion.

The date of the earliest Phoenician inscriptions in the Mediterranean is also disputed. Inscriptions in Phoenician in the central Mediterranean (on Crete and in Sardinia), which I date to about 1000 B.C.E.—that is, to the end of the 11th century—Greek scholars wish to date later. They are supported in this opinion by a few West Semitic epigraphists (I would not call them paleographers). Classicists resent the notion that Phoenicians preceded the Greeks in this part of the world—despite the fact that their beloved classical sources claim that the Phoenicians were in the West first, followed much later by the Greeks.

The discussion is confused by the issue of colonization. Systematic colonization by the Phoenicians probably did not begin before the ninth century B.C.E. But Phoenician sailors and metallurgists plied the Mediterranean from Cyprus to the Pillars of Hercules beginning no later than the 11th century and left inscribed monuments to mark their passing.

Two inscriptions from the Mediterranean use the same script typologically that is found in late 11th-century inscriptions from Syria-Palestine.[8] *Ad hoc* arguments are made by scholars wishing to date these Phoenician inscriptions from the Mediterranean late. Usually they suggest a lag in the development of the script; that is, the script in these two inscriptions, they contend, occupied a peripheral pocket that preserved an ancient hand intact for centuries.

But the argument makes no sense. For one thing the inscriptions are found in port towns where continued contact with the Phoenician merchants and seamen should have updated script styles regularly. Further, and decisively, a pocket of peripheral archaism can not exist unless the Phoenicians had a presence in the Mediterranean from the 11th century until the putative time of the "lagging" script.

Sooner or later, I believe, classicists will be forced to move the date of the borrowing of the alphabet back. Certainly a date in the seventh century, the old standard view of Greek scholars, is now impossible to defend.[9] At present the debate is really between the ninth century and the 11th century. The older date, I feel certain, will prevail.[10]

HS: Did the invention of the alphabet in any way contribute to Israel's spiritual progress? This was also the very place where spiritual inventions, if you will, were made. Do you see any connection there?

FMC: I think so. At least the case can be made. Israel was among the first of the alphabetic nations. There were others, particularly the Phoenicians and the Greeks. Once you move into the period when the alphabet was in intense use, you find evidence of more rigorous ways of thinking, more logical ways of thinking, more critical ways of thinking, more systematic ways of thinking. This is obvious in Greece where we find emerging syllogistic reasoning and systematic logical classification and, later, the full flowering of philosophy and skepticism. One can debate how important a role the alphabet played. But certainly it played a role.

On the other hand, we know little about Phoenician intellectual life. We do know that the pre-Socratic philosophers of the Milesian school were influenced in their cosmological speculation by Phoenician lore and Egyptian cosmological lore mediated by Phoenicians. William F. Albright, in an important paper, the last from his pen, discusses the debt of the Greeks to the Phoenicians. He remarks also that in the Hebrew Bible we find rare approaches to systematic classification and to formalized propositions.[11]

However, it is in the critique of society that we find Israel's genius. Socrates and Amos, each in his own way, were both critics of society. I find it difficult to conceive of the prophetic movement in Israel, with its radical critique of society, apart from a process of the democratization of society and the desacralization of institutions. Greece and Israel are new, radical, "hot" societies. They mark a profound break from the older conservative and hierarchical societies of the ancient

SERĀBÎṬ EL-KHÂDEM, the ancient Egyptian mining site in west central Sinai. The Egyptians were lured to Sinai by turquoise, a semiprecious blue-green stone from which artisans fashioned amulets, scarabs and necklaces. The earliest Egyptian mines in Sinai date to about 2650 B.C.E., but during the XIIth Dynasty (1991-1786 B.C.E.) they moved their operations to the rich veins at Serābîṭ. The photo above shows the inside of a mine.

Serābîṭ el-Khâdem was in operation for more than 800 years and is the site of some of the most magnificent ruins in the entire Sinai peninsula. The remains of a temple dedicated to the goddess Hathor still stand on a plateau overlooking the mines; one of the names by which Hathor was known is "Lady of the Turquoise." (Hathor, with her trademark hairdo, is depicted in the foreground of the bottom photo.) The temple started as a cave where the goddess was worshiped; over the centuries, a portico, chambers, halls, courtyards, pylons and many rooms were added.

INSCRIPTIONS ON THE MINE WALLS at Serābîṭ el-Khâdem. Written in the earliest known alphabetic script, these inscriptions are the single richest source of information about the first alphabet, from which all others derive. Based on the acrophonic principle (see p. 62), that script is called Old Canaanite or proto-Canaanite script (although in the form found at Serābîṭ it is known as proto-Sinaitic). Sir Flinders Petrie, widely considered the father of modern Near Eastern archaeology, found ten such inscriptions in 1905.

Scholars disagree about how the inscriptions at Serābîṭ el-Khâdem should be read, although they generally agree on the identity of most of the letters. The two photos (below and bottom right) and the drawing show a 26-letter inscription (written in a continuous L-shape, with symbols 17 and 18 side by side). Several objects are easily recognizable: an ox head (letters 1, 11, 20, 23), which evolved into the Hebrew letter *ʾalep* and our *a*; a snake (2), the precursor of *nun* and *n*; a

fish (7), forerunner of *dalet* and *d*; the sign for water
(9, 14, 18, 21), the source for *mem* and *m*; and a man's
head (22, 24), the precursor of *reš* and *r*. William
Albright deciphered the inscription to read
"Thou, O Shaphan, collect from ʾAbaba eight(?)
minas (of turquoise). Shimeʿa, groom of the
chief of the car[avaneers(?)]."

A stone plaque (right) inscribed
with an ox head and a crooked staff,
the forerunner of *lamed*, reads "ʾEl,"
the principal north Semitic deity and
one of the names for God in the
Hebrew Bible.

Despite general disagreement over
how to read the Serābît el-Khâdem inscriptions, the meaning of one frequently occurring
word is undisputed. The word is *lbʿlt* (l-ba-al-at),
"to Baʿalat," the feminine form of the Semitic word
meaning "Lord." The frequent appearance of the name
of a Semitic deity on inscriptions at an Egyptian mining site
in Sinai indicates that Semites were present at the site, probably in large numbers and probably as skilled workmen. Many scholars believe that the Semitic workmen at Serābît worshiped Baʿalat in the form of Hathor in the vast temple found
on the site.

The Serābît el-Khâdem inscriptions, dated by Flinders Petrie (and confirmed by
other researchers) to about 1500 B.C.E., were the earliest known examples of proto-
Canaanite script until recently, when a few inscriptions dating to the 16th century
or earlier were found in what was Canaan.

Near East. I have little doubt that the invention of the alphabet and its increasing use played a role in the emergence of these changes.

HS: Did the environment, the richness of different cultures interacting, enable Israel to produce spiritual insights?

FMC: I think so, although I am not sure I would use the term spiritual. The prophetic insights had to do with justice, with egalitarianism, with the redemption of the poor and oppressed, with the evils and self-interest of the powerful, with the corruption of court and temple. Israel arose as the ancient, brilliant cultures of Mesopotamia and Egypt had become decadent or moribund. They were always "cold" societies, static, hierarchical, oppressive. They had their season, and the ancient world was ripe for change.

HS: What would you describe as new in Israel?

FMC: Israel's critique of kingship and temple. The prophets do not spare the priesthood and the temple in their resounding judgments on Israel. Jeremiah tells priests and people that the Temple of Yahweh will not protect them, that it is not inviolable sacred space. The prophets never permitted kingship in Israel to become an Oriental despotism. There were always limits on the

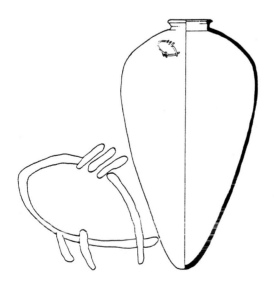

PISCINE SYMBOLS representing the letter *dag* (which means "fish") appear near the necks of two 16th-century B.C.E. storage jars discovered at Gezer, in central Israel. These and 11 other symbols from the Gezer jars, seven of which have been positively identified, are the earliest known examples of proto-Canaanite script, the first alphabet. The letter *dag* later came to be known as *dalet*, the fourth letter of Canaanite and related alphabets (including Hebrew).

king. The prophets refused to leave the kings in peace.

HS: A kind of constitutional monarchy?

FMC: I think we can call Israel's monarchy a limited monarchy. The legal traditions of the old tribal league, not the decrees of the king, remained normative in theory, if not in fact. The kings, beginning with Solomon, tried to assume absolute power in the manner of monarchs elsewhere in the ancient Near East. But the people and their prophetic leaders insisted that kingship was late and provisional in Israel.

The ninth century B.C.E. was marked by the so-called prophetic revolution. The issue was two opposing systems of land tenure—the old traditions of the league, which held that land held as a patrimony was inalienable, versus a (Canaanite) royal system of land grants, especially those given to aging military leaders who had been stalwarts of the standing army.

These threatened to become a landed aristocracy that "added house to house and field to field." The episode of Naboth's vineyard (1 Kings 21) became the *cause célèbre*. Ahab attempted to buy Naboth's vineyard. Naboth refused to sell explaining that the vineyard was part of his patrimony and hence inalienable. Jezebel, daughter of the king of Tyre, bride of Ahab, arranged that Naboth be executed on trumped up charges of treason and blasphemy, and the vineyard was subsequently seized as crown property. The upshot of the conflict symbolized by the vineyard was the violent revolution of Jehu that brought to an end the dynasty of Omri and Ahab.

HS: What about Israel's insights into the nature of the deity?

FMC: The religions of Israel's neighbors were sophisticated, tolerant polytheisms with universal gods usually reflecting the powers of nature. They differed little from the religions of Greece and Rome, and when East and West came into contact, the gods of one pantheon were quickly and easily identified with their equivalents in the other. A fundamental mythic pattern in Canaan and Mesopotamia describes the cosmos as emerging from theomachy, a conflict among the gods, in which kingship in heaven—and hence on earth—is established by the victory of the storm god, the god of fertility and life. Human society participates in these orders of creation because kingship on earth was rooted in divine kingship, which was properly unchanging and eternal.

The social metaphors that shaped Israel's early religion were, so to speak, "premonarchic." Kingship, as we have noted, was suspect in Israel, provisional in the view of old-fashioned Yahwists. Israel's society was structured by kinship, especially in the early period, and its tribal society developed into a confederated league of tribes; kinship was extended by legal fiction, that is, by covenant. Leagues were considered to be at once kinship groups, tracing their lineage to a putative ancestor, linking the tribes with more or less artificial, segmented genealogies and, at the same time, covenanted leagues, the covenant extending the duties, obligations and privileges of kinship to all members of the league.

There were a number of such leagues in the south—Edom, Ammon, Moab, Midian and the Arab leagues, notably Qedar. Characteristically, the leagues were named for patron gods conceived as Divine Kinsmen or as covenant gods who took upon themselves the duties of kinship to their kindred, the members of the league, or (to say the same thing) to their covenant partners.

Israel's league was called the kindred of Yahweh (ʿam yahweh). In Ammon the tribal society was the kindred of Milkom, in Edom the kindred of Qos, in Moab, the kindred of Chemosh, in North Arabia the kindred or family of ʿAthtar-shamayn (ʾahl ʿAthtar-šamayn). The cult of each tribal league centered on one god, the league patron, the Divine Kinsman who led the league in migration and especially in war and whose law governed relations between league elements.

The onomasticon (inventory of personal names) of each of these kinship societies in the south was dominated by theophoric names (names with a divine element), in which the league god is called upon. In Israel the onomasticon is dominated by Yahweh or ʾEl; in Ammon, by Milkom (see photo and drawing on p. 83) or ʾEl. The names Milkom and Yahweh originated, evidently, as epithets of ʾEl, the patriarch of the gods. In Moab names are compounded with Chemosh, an epithet of ʿAthtar/ʿAštar; in Edom, with Qos, probably a cultic name of Haddu/Hadad.

This onomastic practice in the leagues of the south contrasts vividly with the usage in the Canaanite city-states, as well as in

Mesopotamia, where the whole pantheon of high gods is called upon in the theophoric names in their onomasticon.

The Divine Kinsman is a type of deity originating in patriarchal religion, called by Albrecht Alt the "god of the father," the forerunner, typologically, of the league god. This is not to say that the cult of the god of the father or the league god was monotheistic, either in early Israel or in the leagues of the south. But in Israel the claims of their jealous god can be described as a *praeparatio* for the later development of monotheism in Israel. Israel's league god was its primary patron and demanded an exclusive league cultus. At some point, Yahweh alone was seen as having significant power and sovereignty. The other gods lost their powers. If other gods have no real power, they are of no interest religiously, and so, from that point on, one may speak of existential monotheism in Israel.

HS: The others are non-gods?

FMC: To go from gods with little power to non-gods is, I guess, a philosophical leap of considerable distance. "Dead gods," oddly, continued to play a role in Israel. The god of Israel still possessed a proper name, Yahweh. He was not simply God. The elements of nature continued long to be confronted as "Thou" rather than "it." Still, it was in Israel that monotheism emerged. Evidently, the social structures and cultural currents that marked Israelite society provided a matrix for the birth of monotheism.

We assume that, in other nation states that originated in leagues, the old social and religious forms broke down; kingship there too replaced the older league traditions—and polytheism flourished. In Israel, however, largely because of the prophetic movement and its egalitarian ideals, the hierarchical institutions of kingship were never wholly successful in extirpating institutions and concepts rooted in the old league society.

The ideology of kingship—kingship established in heaven and coeval with creation and cosmos—never fully prevailed in Israel in the era of kings. Israel's kings were not divine, at least not in prophetic eyes. Rather, strange to say, the Mosaic Age, that is, the era of the league, was considered the normative or ideal age. The great literary figures in Israel did not look to David and his successors for formulations of Israel's religion and law. They looked back to an older time and older institutions and idealized them.

The Deuteronomist in the seventh century B.C.E., and the Priestly source of the Tetrateuch (Genesis, Exodus, Leviticus and Numbers) in the sixth century B.C.E., attempted to reconstruct systematically the institutions and law of the Age of Moses—as a basis for reform in the case of the Deuteronomist and, in the case of the Priestly tradent (the receiver, shaper and transmitter of tradition), for reconstituting the exiled community in a future return to Zion.

Earlier, when Baʿalism—that is, Canaanite polytheism—threatened to prevail in Israel, most powerfully in the ninth century B.C.E. during the reign of the kings of the Omride dynasty, a war broke out between the great prophets, on the one hand, and the court and its syncretists, on the other. The prophets and their jealous deity won. Later, under the onslaught of Assyria, Babylon, Persia, Macedonia and Rome, the nations round about Israel in effect disappear, leaving little imprint of their culture or religion.

The survival of Israel in Exile and under foreign rule for centuries thereafter is a remarkable phenomenon. Certain gigantic figures of the sixth century, several anonymous, are responsible for preserving and transforming Israel's historic faith. They played an important role

in the survival of Israel as a national community. In the Exilic period the basic scriptures were codified and put into writing in penultimate or final form. It was a period of unrivaled literary creativity.

HS: Who were these gigantic figures?

FMC: There is the Priestly tradent—one or more—who edited and supplemented the old Epic sources to bring the whole Tetrateuch to completion. By the time of the return of the exiles to Jerusalem in the late sixth century B.C.E., the work was probably complete; certainly it was complete by the time of Ezra (early fifth century), to whom tradition credits the definitive edition.

The Exilic Deuteronomist, another gigantic figure, put Deuteronomy and the Deuteronomistic history (Joshua, Judges, Samuel and Kings) into final form.[12]

There was also the strange but brilliant prophet Ezekiel and his school, and, above all, the literary and religious genius we label Second Isaiah whose work includes Isaiah 40-55 and probably 34-35. Second Isaiah, with good reason, has been called the savior of his nation and its faith. He reinterpreted the faith in a way that came to terms with the trauma of the Exile and gave hope for the future, declaring that

EARLY GREEK INSCRIPTION. Carved into a mountainside, this inscription from the Aegean island of Thera (also known as Santorini) is one of the earliest known inscriptions in Greek. The first line (read left to right) reads ΘΑΡΗΣ (Tharēs), while the second (read right to left) reads ΑΝΑΣΙΚΛΗΣ (Anasiklēs).

Scholars disagree about when the Greeks adopted the Semitic alphabet. Professor Cross believes the transmission occurred earlier rather than later—in the 11th century B.C.E., as opposed to the ninth century as is argued by some scholars. The seventh-century date, the old date upheld by many classicists, has been superseded.

Cross cites several reasons to support an 11th-century date. First, the earliest Greek writing was multidirectional, that is, it could be written from right to left, left to right, *both* right to left and left to right (writing known as boustrophedon, "as the ox ploughs"), or vertically. The same was true of Phoenician writing until the middle of the 11th century B.C.E. (the Phoenician alphabet was the successor of Old Canaanite writing). By the second half of the 11th century, the Greek and Phoenician scripts parted ways—literally. Greek became fixed in the left-to-right direction, and Phoenician stabilized in the right-to-left direction. If the Greeks had absorbed the alphabet from the Phoenicians after the 11th century, Cross reasons, they would also have adopted the Phoenician direction of writing. He also points out that the earliest Greek writings stand in elegant continuity with the 11th-century inscribed arrowheads (see p. 66).

Israel's universal, prophetic vocation would be fulfilled in new mighty acts of Israel's God. Our edition of Job, too, is to be dated in the Exilic period. In his dialogues the poet struggles with the problem of justice and concludes with a pessimistic answer. In Job, only mystery speaks from the thunderstorm.

Second Isaiah takes up Job's notion of the hidden god who is all mystery. He provides a basis for once again having faith that God rules justly in history. He does not cover up or explain away innocent suffering and injustice in past events. Rather, Second Isaiah creates an eschatology that illuminates history and provides a basis for hope. And, in sublime poetry, he creates his new epic of Israelite history and world history.

HS: Are you suggesting that the Exilic Deuteronomist and the Priestly tradent worked in exile in Babylonia?

FMC: The Deuteronomist was probably a Jew left behind in Jerusalem. I am inclined to believe that the Priestly tradent belonged to the exiled community in Babylon. Ezekiel was certainly in Babylon (despite a few scholars who argue for a Jerusalem locale or at least for a Jerusalem

THE NORA FRAGMENT was discovered in the 19th century on the island of Sardinia. This 18-inch-high by 24-inch-wide stone slab contains the remains of an inscription written in Phoenician-style Semitic letters. Epigraphers are strongly divided over the date of the inscription. Professor Cross believes it was written boustrophedon-style ("as the ox ploughs," that is, alternating between right to left and left to right) and dates it to about 1000 B.C.E. If Cross is correct, the Nora Fragment is the oldest Semitic inscription from the central or western Mediterranean and bolsters his theory that the Phoenician alphabet was disseminated much earlier than many classicists have thought.

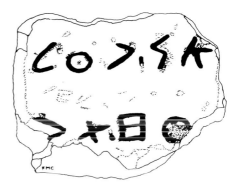

visit), and the Priestly lore and point of view is closely allied to Ezekiel's. They belong to the same school, in my opinion.

HS: Why did the editors of the Deuteronomistic history, especially the author of the first edition from the time of Josiah, turn back to the Mosaic period for inspiration?

FMC: I believe that the impulse stems from the prophetic tradition, especially the tradition that survives from northern Israel, and also from the circles in rural areas (as opposed to the royal establishment in Jerusalem) that maintained elements of the old kinship institutions and covenantal law despite royal rule.

HS: But why the Deuteronomistic reform in the time of Josiah? There were kings before him and after him.

FMC: Hezekiah did try a similar reform in the late eighth century.

HS: Yes. You have two religious reforms—Hezekiah's reform and Josiah's reform—and both failed.

FMC: Both reforms were inspired by Deuteronomistic ideology. This ideology appears to have affinities with Hosea and northern circles and became a strong influence on the Judahite court after the northern kingdom, Israel, was overrun and annexed by Assyria in the late eighth century. Refugees from the north flowed into the southern kingdom, Judah, at this time.

The reforms of Hezekiah in the late eighth century and of Josiah in the late seventh century were not merely religious. They also reflected a strong nationalistic impulse. Hezekiah and Josiah were both attempting to reestablish the united kingdom of David in all its glory. They made efforts to re-take the northern kingdom, partitioned in their time into three Assyrian provinces, and to unify the state and its national cultus in Jerusalem.

The program to reestablish the Davidic empire and to unify its national cultus was not forgotten, even after Josiah's time. John Hyrcanus I (134-104 B.C.E.) made an ambitious attempt in this direction, destroying the Samaritan temple and requiring all who wished to remain in his realm—including Samaritans and Idumeans—to convert to orthodox (i.e., Jerusalemite) Judaism. Almost certainly Zerubbabel, the Davidic governor of Judah in the late sixth century, made a bid to carry out a major reform. It was he who completed the building of the Second Temple. He disappears abruptly from history, and the rule of Judah passes to non-Davidic appointees of the Persian crown. The easiest explanation of our limited data is to suppose that Zerubbabel's political as well as religious program brought Persian wrath down on him and that the Persian crown, contrary to its usual practice of appointing local nobility to exercise hereditary rule, dared not permit another Davidic figure to become governor.

HS: *The Deuteronomistic history consists of Deuteronomy and the books of Joshua, Judges, Samuel and Kings?*

FMC: Yes, at least the second edition includes the books you have listed. It is not certain when Deuteronomy was combined with the remainder of the history.

HS: *How do you distinguish the first edition of the Deuteronomistic history from the second?*

FMC: There are two lines of argument in the Deuteronomistic history, which are in the strongest tension, if not contradictory. One is that the hope for the future, the restoration of a unified nation and a pure, single cultus, which rests in the reservoir of grace created by the fidelity of David, lies concretely in Josiah of the house of David, whose reform is destined to restore Mosaic and Davidic institutions. This hope belongs to the time of the Josianic program (late seventh century) and makes sense only as propaganda for the reform. The other line of argument in the Deuteronomistic history is that time has run out. Jerusalem and its Temple are marked for destruction, and there is no hope, no means of salvation. This theme presumes the fall of Jerusalem and the Exile. The late edition of the Deuteronomistic history is updated from Josiah to the Exile.

The basic argument of the first edition of this history, so basic that it could not be eradicated, was that the promises to David would be fulfilled in Josiah. In the most flagrant instance of *vaticinium ex*

AMMONITE SEAL IMPRESSION. A scarab beetle with four outstretched wings occupies the middle third of an Ammonite seal impression from about 600 B.C.E. The impression (photo above and drawing below) was discovered in 1984 at Tell el-'Umeiri, in Jordan, 37 miles east of Jerusalem. A two-line inscription, above and below the scarab, reads *lmlkm'wr 'bd b'lys'*. The excavators translated it as, "Belonging to Milkom'ur, servant of Ba'alyiš'a." Milkom was the god of the Ammonites, and the owner's name probably means "Milkom's Flame" or "Milkom is flame." This is the first known Ammonite name containing the divine element. The Ba'alyiš'a whom Milkom'ur served is most likely the Ammonite king Baalis mentioned in Jeremiah 40:14. Professor Cross notes that ancient Israel was a trib-

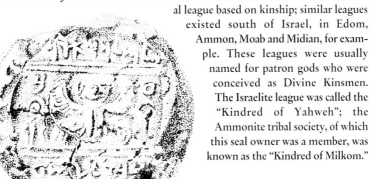

al league based on kinship; similar leagues existed south of Israel, in Edom, Ammon, Moab and Midian, for example. These leagues were usually named for patron gods who were conceived as Divine Kinsmen. The Israelite league was called the "Kindred of Yahweh"; the Ammonite tribal society, of which this seal owner was a member, was known as the "Kindred of Milkom."

eventu (prophecy after the event) to be found in the Hebrew Bible, the historian of the first edition actually puts into the mouth of a ninth-century prophet the prophecy that the altar of Bethel, symbol of the cult that stood as the rival of Jerusalem, would be destroyed by one to be born of the house of David, Josiah by name (1 Kings 13:1-2; cf. 2 Kings 23:15-16). This was, of course, written in the late seventh century B.C.E. in Josiah's own time.

The secondary argument, found in light reworkings of the first edition of the Deuteronomistic history, turns this history into a lawsuit against Israel for violations of the covenant, which inevitably, ineluctably, bring destruction and exile as punishment. Josiah comes too late. Doom has already been determined. God's verdict against Israel has already been given. The second edition arbitrarily decides that it is Manasseh's apostasy that was ultimately unforgivable. The sermon against Samaria (2 Kings 17, especially verses 7-23) recounting the sins that decreed the destruction of the northern kingdom in the eighth century, is plagiarized by the Exilic Deuteronomist and applied to Manasseh; as so applied, these sins ensure the fall of the southern kingdom, Judah.

The procedure of the Exilic Deuteronomist is curious. From a historical point of view, Solomon makes a much more plausible candidate than Manasseh—or the last kings of Judah might have been chosen—on whom to hang these sins. By using Manasseh, the Exilic Deuteronomist must suppress the story of Manasseh's repentance (preserved in 2 Chronicles 33). And, in making Manasseh the culprit, the Exilic Deuteronomist makes the whole attempt at reform on the part of Josiah an exercise in futility. It is interesting, however, that the Exilic Deuteronomist places blame for the fall of Jerusalem in the relatively distant past. It is not the fault of his own generation. His generation could do nothing; the exiles paid for the sins of their fathers.

Ezekiel in exile gives a similar, and even more remarkable, explanation of the destruction of the kingdoms of Israel and Judah (Ezekiel 20:19-26). The fault, Ezekiel says, rests in the generation who revolted in the wilderness. Yahweh swore an oath in the days when Israel was still in the wilderness that he would scatter the children of Israel among the nations—in exile. Further, the deity in Ezekiel's oracle explains that he gave to Israel laws that were "not good" and ordinances to insure that they would not live. In effect, Israel was damned even before the monarchy was initiated, half a millennium and more before Jerusalem and the Temple fell. This is a most radical explanation of the cause of the Exile. Ezekiel is a radical book and barely made it into the canon.

At the end of this interview, Professor Cross and I talked about his plans for the future. He has a breathtaking collection of orchid plants, some of which are always in bloom, which, he said, would take more of his time. He was also putting the finishing touches on a book of essays, a kind of sequel to his Canaanite Myth and Hebrew Epic.

I asked him what he thought he would do after the essays.

"I will go epigraphic," he said. "For the time I have left, I want to do epigraphy. I would like to do a major synthetic work—if my powers don't completely fade—on paleography from the invention of the alphabet to the Bar Kokhba period (2nd century C.E.*). I have worked in every period—in Hebrew, Phoenician, Aramaic and related scripts. I have notebook after notebook—photographs, drawings and related material. I would like finally to put together my own synthesis.*

"Epigraphy is the field in which I've had the most fun—not textual criticism, not the history of the religion of Israel, not Northwest Semitic grammar. I love deciphering inscriptions; I love paleographical analysis. These are my avocations as well as my vocation. I hope to spend my last years doing what I like best. This may not be the most important thing in the field I have worked in, but it will be something that I will simply enjoy. And I think here I do have something special to transmit."

SAMARIA PAPYRUS I

Caption on page 88.

CHAPTER 4

SEALS AND
OTHER WRITINGS

HS: Let's talk about your interest in early seals and seal impressions. This has been a favorite interest of yours, hasn't it?

FMC: Yes, epigraphy has always been a favorite subject of mine, and ancient seals and bullae are a major source of ancient inscriptions. Leather and papyrus documents rarely survive from biblical times. Seals, cut usually from precious or semiprecious stones, are virtually indestructible. Bullae (sealings) also survive, being made out of a compound substance that includes clay and a binder. In the biblical period, for the most part, they consist of very short inscriptions, usually the name and patronymic of the bearer and sometimes the owner's occupation—scribe, steward, mayor of the city, governor, prefect. Seals on rings or seals hung from a string around the neck were used to seal documents, particularly legal documents, in antiquity.

This practice still survives in certain contexts, again particularly in making legal documents official. Notary publics still use seals. But rarely do we have a seal ring or a necklace seal to use when we buy a slave, get married or buy a house. In biblical antiquity, parties to legal transactions and witnesses, often including a king, a governor or his prefect, before whom the transaction was executed, and the scribe who wrote the document, affixed their seals. Sealings were, in effect, official signatures.

Earlier, in the Late Bronze Age (1550-1200 B.C.E.) and the beginning of the Iron Age (1200-586 B.C.E.), most seals were anepigraphic (without inscriptions), nonrepresentational decorations. This is not because the Canaanites and early Israelites were unable to write, as some have suggested; it was a matter of fashion. We have many inscribed arrowheads from the 11th century B.C.E., a fad of the period—but not inscribed seals. In the Exilic period (586-538 B.C.E.) and Persian period (538-331 B.C.E.) in Palestine, seals reverted to scenes—persons, mythical creatures, animals. In this period literacy was obviously widespread in Palestine.

We have an inscribed seal or two that antedates the eighth century. However, in the course of the eighth century the practice of using inscribed seals became immensely popular. Inscribed seals from Egypt and Mesopotamia were well known in earlier periods, but the Israelites took up the fashion in earnest only in the eighth, seventh and early sixth centuries. In the early eighth century, a person of property or means had a seal or seals with his name inscribed on them, and usually a glyptic representation; in the seventh and early sixth century, inhabitants of Judah almost always had seals of two panels where name and patronymic were inscribed, with, at most, lines or nonrepresentative decorations. It has been suggested that the traditional law against icons of deity had hardened at this time to include most pictorial art. In any case, carving representations of human beings, animals or mythological beings, or decorations with astral symbols or cult objects had gone out of fashion, by and large, until the Persian period when seals were again mostly pictorial.

SAMARIA PAPYRUS 1, page 86. In 1962, Taʿâmireh bedouin found 300 skeletons and a handful of badly worn papyrus business documents in a cave in Wâdī ed-Dâliyeh. The skeletons are believed to be the remains of rebels against the rule of Alexander the Great who took refuge in the cave, where they met a grisly end. When their pursuers discovered their hideout, they built a large fire at the cave entrance suffocating everyone inside.

The documents date from about 375 B.C.E. to 335 B.C.E. Some of the papyri contain references to specific regnal years, which helps scholars establish the dates of scripts. Among the Samaria papyri were several bullae, or sealings. In the one shown, the messenger of the gods, Hermes, wearing a chlamys (a short woolen mantle), clutches a caduceus (herald's staff). Representations of humans, animals or mythological figures were popular on bullae during the Persian period (late sixth to fourth century B.C.E.).

There are exceptions in the Persian period. High officials, priests and governors sometimes put their names on undecorated seals. A sealing (bulla) with the name of "Sanballaṭ the governor of Samaria" on a papyrus found in the Wâdī ed-Dâliyeh is an example. Ordinary people in the Persian period, to judge particularly from Samarian finds, did not have seals inscribed with their names. They had seals with carved pictures only.

HS: Did ordinary people have seals?

FMC: I am sure that everyone but the lowest strata of society had seals. We have some seals that are excessively crude and badly engraved—not the exquisite work of the professional engravers. Anyone with official business, anyone who wrote letters, anyone who bought a house or field or slave, anyone who was involved in legal transactions had a personal seal. Trained scribes usually were called upon to write legally binding documents; then the document, usually papyrus, was rolled up and bullae attached.

I should add that the large corpus of names from seals and bullae have made interesting studies in onomastics, the history of name usage and formation. Since the names usually contain religious sentiments and the name of the national god (especially in Israel, Moab, Edom and Ammon—nation states that arose as tribal leagues bound to patron gods), they are good resources for the historical study of the religions of these peoples.

HS: What about monumental inscriptions in Israel?

FMC: Oddly, we have more monumental inscriptions from Ammon and from Moab in Transjordan—not to mention Phoenicia or the Aramaean city states—than we do from Israel. Ironically, the newly discovered stele from Dan mentioning the House of David is a ninth-century B.C.E. Aramaic victory stele, probably celebrating a victory over Israel by Damascene forces. We do have a few Hebrew inscriptions of monumental size. But their rarity, given the archaeological exploitation of Israel, is astonishing, not to say eerie—as if there were a conspiracy, divine or human, to withhold contemporary sources that might supplement (or correct) the biblical story.

SEAL OF MIQNÊYAW. The two-line inscription on this highly polished red jasper seal reads "Belonging to Miqnêyaw, servant of Yahweh" (*lmqnyw ʿbd yhwh*). Dated to the first half of the eighth century B.C.E., this half-inch-long and quarter-inch-wide seal contains the oldest known reference to the Israelite deity on an ancient Hebrew seal. The top drawing shows the inscription as it appears on the seal above. Only when the seal was pressed into wet clay could the mirror image letters be read correctly. The lower drawing shows the inscription on the back of the seal. This inscription is in the correct orientation. It reads *mqnyw ʿbd yhwh* (in the correct orientation), without the prefix *l*, meaning "belonging to." A longitudinal perforation through the seal indicates that it was meant to hang from a string.

Who was Miqnêyaw? The name is a variant of Miqneyahu, one of 12 singer/musicians who accompanied the Ark of the Covenant to the City of David (1 Chronicles 15:18,21). The name Miqnêyaw means either "creature of Yahweh" or "property of Yahweh." The title "servant of Yahweh," based on West Semitic parallels, suggests that the individual so designated served some sacral function. In a study of this seal, Professor Cross theorized that Miqnêyaw was not an obscure temple functionary, but a great cantor of early Israel.

There is, I believe, an explanation for the paucity of monumental inscriptions. In recent years, monumental inscriptions painted on plaster (*dipinti*) have turned up at Kuntillet ʿAjrûd in Sinai and at Deir ʿAllā in Gilead (in Transjordan). There is, moreover, a biblical account of Moses prescribing, and Joshua fulfilling, directions to take standing stones (*maṣṣebôt*), smooth the surfaces, apply plaster, write upon them Israel's laws, and set them up for public display in a sanctuary in the vicinity of Shechem (Deuteronomy 27:1-8 and Joshua 8:30-35).

In excavations in Israel, many smoothed standing stones have turned up, some with remnants of plaster on them, which obviously served some public or cultic purpose. If they had plaster on them and inscriptions painted on the plaster, the centuries have washed away the writing and most or all of the plaster. Apparently, the fashion of writing on plaster, rather than engraving in stone, has robbed us of surviving monumental inscriptions. At least this is a theory I have long held. Recently, Lawrence Stager, my colleague at Harvard, actually found evidence of the practice at Carthage. There many stelae of the *tophet* (the precinct of child sacrifice) were plastered and inscribed, but in the course of time, the plaster and writing has almost, but not entirely, eroded away.

To return to our discussion of the seals, I have always been fascinated by the typology of name usage, the historical fashions of name formation. In the first paper I ever published,[1] in 1947, I challenged the argument that the names in the Priestly strata of the Pentateuch were made up, fabricated in the post-Exilic period. Now, the patterns of name formation found in early names recorded in the Priestly strata of the Pentateuch are so well documented in early Israel that it is absurd to argue they are spurious.

There is an interesting pattern in the use of the element ʾEl in Hebrew names. In earliest Israel, names with the element ʾEl (god) or the proper name ʾEl are very popular, indeed ubiquitous. Later, names with the theophorous element Yahū or Yaw (apocopated forms of Yahweh) replace the ʾEl names in popularity. Then there is a resurgence of ʾEl names in the Persian, Hellenistic and Roman periods. This curious resurgence of the use of names compounded with ʾEl misled generations of biblical scholars who assumed, on the basis of unilinear evolution, that names compounded with ʾEl were late. Hence the appearance of ʾEl names early in the Priestly Code were considered anachronistic—fictional. Onomastic studies give hard evidence from extrabiblical sources. They correct the presuppositions of scholars confined to internal analysis of biblical lore, scholars who contrive simple, unilinear, evolutionary models of histories of Israel and Israelite religion.

I am also interested in the history of spelling. Spelling fashions can also be arranged in a typology and dated. Like the script itself, in pre-Exilic inscriptions and seals in Hebrew, Phoenician, Aramaic, Ammonite, Moabite and Edomite—the West Semitic dialects and national script styles—the fashion in spelling steadily evolved. Early, in Aramaic, the first vowel letters, *matres lectionis*, were introduced to mark final long vowels. Initially, only the letters *yod*, *waw* and *he* were used to mark vowels. They were used regularly in Aramaic, and later in Hebrew and Transjordanian dialects, to mark final long vowels and sporadically to mark internal long vowels. In Phoenician, where a conservative scribal tradition prevailed, these vowel markers were

THE NORA STONE. Discovered in 1773 in Nora, a city on the southern coast of Sardinia, this 3.5-foot-high and nearly 2-foot-wide slab bears an eight-line inscription in Semitic letters written Phoenician style (right to left). Professor Cross believes there once were two additional lines at the top.

The inscription begins "at Tarshish," a common place-name derived from a Semitic root meaning "to smelt." Tarshish may have been a Phoenician mining town in Sardinia. The inscription continues "and he drove them out./Among the Sardinians he is [now] at peace, / (and) his army is at peace: / Milkatōn son of / Šubnaʾ, general/ of (king) Pummay." Pummay, also written Puʿmyatōn and known in Greek as Pygmalion, ruled Tyre from 831 to 785 B.C.E. Based on Pummay's dates and the shape and stance of the letters, Cross dates the Nora Stone inscription to 825 B.C.E. He believes the Phoenicians sent an army to Sardinia that year to quell a local revolt and protect their mining interests in the area.

not used at all until Late Punic times (third to second centuries B.C.E.).

The fashion of using vowel letters in Hebrew changed over the centuries. Early *matres lectionis* were used almost exclusively to mark final long vowels. Very rarely, particularly in borrowed words and so-called biliteral roots [with two consonants instead of the usual three], they were used to mark internal long vowels. Slowly the use of internal vowel letters and phoneme markers expanded, and later *ʾalep* was added as a vowel letter in Hebrew under the influence of Aramaic once more. The letter *waw*, initially used only to mark long *ü* or *û*, with the contraction of the diphthong *aw* (>*ô*), was extended to mark *ô*, and eventually *ō* derived from *ā*. A typology of spelling styles over the centuries can be described, a key, like the study of script styles and grammatical development, to date inscriptions.

Now, to complicate matters, scribes copying early and late biblical documents wrote in the paleographic, grammatical and orthographic styles of their own time. Later scribes tended to modernize each of these styles but not always systematically. Sometimes they even modernized the lexicon as words grew obsolete or developed scatological or obscene secondary meanings. For example, in one context (1 Samuel 20:34), Saul's son Jonathan is said to jump up from the table in excitement. The verb meaning "to rise in excitement" (*wypḥz*) developed an obscene secondary meaning one might guess, "to become tumescent," and was changed in the traditional text to the common term, "to arise" (*wyqm*). The original wording survives in the old Samuel manuscript from Qumrân Cave 4 (4QSam[b]) and in the Old Greek translation. The failure of the scribes to modernize systematically means that archaisms still survive, especially in archaic contexts and poetry, which resists modernization. A kind of palimpsest effect may result giving keys to the original date of documents.

Paleography has been a typological discipline I have pursued at almost every stage of the script, from the origins of the Old Canaanite alphabet to its proliferation into national scripts—Aramaic, Hebrew, Phoenician and Greek. In the case of Hebrew, I have described in detail the evolution of script styles from the tenth-century Old Hebrew script derived from the script of the Phoenician chancelleries, to the Jewish and paleo-Hebrew scripts of the era of Bar Kokhba in the second century C.E. In the Hebrew of the era of the kings of Israel, at least two styles evolved, a lapidary script, used especially on seals, and a cursive script that originated in the penned hands of scribes using papyrus and ostraca for writing. Ostraca, inscribed potsherds, used for everyday purposes of writing records and sometimes letters, are numerous in ancient Israelite tells. The modern archaeological method is to dip all potsherds in water and examine them for writing before scrubbing them for cleaning with wire brushes. The result has been a bumper crop of inscriptions found in the last few decades that were missed in earlier digs.

My study of inscriptions, seals and ostraca, as well as leather and papyri and monumental inscriptions in the rare cases where they are preserved, as always is governed by a systematic interest—indeed a passion—for historical typologies—the development of scripts, the evolution of artistic styles on seals, the history of onomastic patterns and usage, the history of spelling, of grammar and of lexicon.

The accumulations of banal bits of technical information on a thousand bits of inscribed pottery, seals and the like slowly builds up into a rich corpus of information for attacking historical, literary and even text-critical problems. I enjoy these detailed and technical labors as long as I can alternate them with more general and humanistic projects.

ISAIAH SCROLL

Caption on page 98.

CHAPTER 5

THE HISTORY AND SIGNIFICANCE OF THE DEAD SEA SCROLLS

HS: Do you remember the first time you heard about the Dead Sea Scrolls?

FMC: Very vividly. It was a dramatic episode in my life. I was sitting in my carrel in the library at Johns Hopkins University where I was a doctoral student in Semitic languages. David Noel Freedman, a fellow student, was sitting nearby. Our teacher, William Foxwell Albright, rushed into the library and told us to come to his office; he had something to show us. He was quite agitated and rushed out. We followed him into his study. There he showed us photographs that had been sent to him from the American School of Oriental Research in Jerusalem. They pictured two columns of a manuscript, columns of the Book of Isaiah. He then began to go over the features of the script of the manuscript, noting each paleographical detail. Before he was done he had dated this manuscript to the second century B.C.E., and more precisely to the second half of the second century. No wonder he radiated excitement.

Noel and I persuaded Albright to let us take the glossy photographs home with us overnight. We spent all night working with them. My wife was ousted from our combination living room/bedroom/study and spent the night sleeping in the bathroom, in a huge Victorian tub roomy enough for her to install a mattress and to sleep more or less comfortably. Noel and I examined the textual readings of the old manuscript, analyzed the unusual spelling (an interest of ours), and, as far as we were able, studied the paleographical features of the manuscript. We spent an extraordinary night with the photographs of what is now labeled 1QIsaᵃ, the great Isaiah Scroll of Qumrân Cave 1.

HS: Do you remember the date?

FMC: It was in the early spring of 1948, in late February or early March.

HS: Were you able to make an independent judgment yourself, apart from what Albright told you?

FMC: Not immediately. Although early Hebrew epigraphy and paleography were of particular interest to me at that time, I had not yet worked systematically on the scripts of the period of the Isaiah Scroll. Within a few days, however, I had studied Albright's paper on the Nash Papyrus,[1] which first fixed the chronology of the late Aramaic and Jewish scripts of this period. The arguments for a second-century date for the scroll, roughly contemporary with the Nash Papyrus, were compelling. I might say that today, after long study, and with the vast amount of new material that has since become available, including dated documents and manuscripts dated by carbon 14 analysis, the date of

ISAIAH SCROLL, page 96. Among the first Dead Sea Scrolls discovered was this copy of Isaiah, which measures 23.5 feet long and contains the entire text of the 66-chapter prophetic book. The scroll is here open to Isaiah 38:8 through 40:28. The second and third lines in the left column may have been the inspiration for founding the Qumrân community: "In the wilderness prepare the way of the Lord…" (Isaiah 40:3). Isaiah was highly regarded by the Qumrân sectarians. At least 20 other copies of the book were found in the Dead Sea caves.

Professor Cross first saw a photo of this Isaiah scroll early in 1948 when he was a graduate student at Johns Hopkins University. William Foxwell Albright, the leading American figure in Bible studies at the time, excitedly showed the photo to Cross and his fellow student, David Noel Freedman. That night, Cross and Freedman, who later left their own marks on biblical scholarship, studied the photo. Based on paleography—the study of the shape and position of letters—Albright had fixed the date of the Isaiah Scroll to the second half of the second century B.C.E.—a date that has since been corroborated by other dated documents and confirmed by carbon 14 testing.

the great Isaiah Scroll has not required revision—it dates to the second half of the second century B.C.E.

HS: What did Albright say to you when he called you into his office?

FMC: He spoke in superlatives. His paleographical analysis was careful and pedantic. But then he spoke of the greatest archaeological discovery of all times. No one had ever supposed that leather or papyrus materials from this early age could be preserved in Palestine; the climate did not permit such preservation. Albright was a man given to superlatives.

HS: When you saw the photographs, did you have any idea that you would spend so much of your life in Dead Sea Scroll research?

FMC: I knew I would be involved in research on these extraordinary new documents; but I had no notion, of course, of the series of finds that would follow. I knew that there was more than the Isaiah Scroll in the finds of what we now call Qumrân Cave 1. I did not dream that I would spend years of my life putting together tiny fragments of manuscripts from later finds, especially from Cave 4, and papyrus fragments from a cave in the Wâdī ed-Dâliyeh.

HS: What was your next contact with the scrolls?

FMC: My first actual work on the Dead Sea Scroll materials came with my appointment in 1953 as a representative of the American Schools of Oriental Research to an international team of scholars to publish the fragmentary scrolls from Cave 4, found in 1952.

HS: So between 1948 and 1953, you really had nothing to do with the scrolls?

FMC: On the contrary, I was very much engaged with the scrolls. I wrote a review of E. L. Sukenik's (archaeologist at the Hebrew University) publication of the Hebrew University scrolls from Qumrân Cave 1 in 1949, and I entered rather vociferously into the debate raging over the scrolls.

HS: What was the debate about?

FMC: Over the date and authenticity of the scrolls. G. R. Driver in England (later Lord Driver, the leading figure in Hebrew studies in England) and Solomon Zeitlin, a professor of Talmud at the Dropsie College in Philadelphia, to name only the leading figures in the discussion, argued for a medieval date for the scrolls. Zeitlin called them a "hoax" but was never clear as to what he meant by a hoax.

HS: Zeitlin thought they were medieval forgeries?

FMC: Yes, and for my defense of their antiquity and authenticity, he called me a dupe of Albright (and later of de Vaux). Finally, in an issue of the *Jewish Quarterly Review*, he called me, not a dupe, but a liar. I was an active part of the conspiracy. A number of my friends wrote me to give congratulations; I had gained new status as an independent scholar in scroll research. I remember long, animated arguments with Zeitlin in scholarly meetings—often outside the halls where we had read papers. The arguments were vociferous but not

THE NASH PAPYRUS. Dating to the second century B.C.E., this fragment was important in establishing the date of the Isaiah Scroll on the basis of the similarity of scripts. The papyrus is probably a liturgical fragment and contains a version of the Decalogue—the Ten Commandments—and part of the *Shema* prayer (Deuteronomy 6:4-5). In several places, especially in the ordering of the "Thou shalt not" commandments, the Nash Papyrus diverges from the Masoretic text, the traditional text of the Hebrew Bible, and agrees instead with the Septuagint, the third- or second-century B.C.E. Greek translation of the Bible. Before the discovery of the Dead Sea Scrolls, the Nash Papyrus was the oldest known biblical fragment.

angry. He was a gentleman. I remember one discussion in which I contended that the jars in which the scrolls were found were of an early type; Zeitlin said old jars may have been used: "It means nothing." I said the carbon 14 date of the linen covering of the scrolls was early. "It means nothing," he said. Then I asked, if the ink were dated early, would he capitulate? His reply was no, the ink could have been saved over the centuries.

Debates over the date of the scrolls colored the early days of my teaching. In 1950, I came to teach at Wellesley College, my first academic post. I shall never forget my introduction to the academic community there. The occasion was a public lecture by a member of the department of which I was a member—Ernest Lacheman, who was best known for his exemplary publications of Nuzi tablets from the collections of the Harvard Semitic Museum. Lacheman attacked the early date of the Dead Sea Scrolls. He dated them to the Christian period. He defended the position of his mentor, Robert Pfeiffer, who held the chair at Harvard to which I was later elected. Pfeiffer himself prudently never published on the subject.

In any event, following the Lacheman lecture, Louise Pettibone Smith, a formidable woman and chairman of our department at Wellesley, stood up and welcomed me to the faculty and announced

ELIEZER L. SUKENIK was the first scholar to set eyes on a Dead Sea Scroll fragment. In November 1947, Sukenik, a professor at the Hebrew University, was shown a scrap of ancient manuscript through the barbed wire that divided Jerusalem during the last days of British rule in Palestine. Sukenik immediately recognized the authenticity of the fragment and made plans to travel to Bethlehem—an Arab city—on the eve of the United Nations vote on the partition of Palestine to purchase the larger scrolls of which the scrap had been a small part. Sukenik's son, Yigael, (who used the pseudonym Yadin), was chief of operations of the Haganah (the underground Jewish army) and advised

him not to go. But Sukenik insisted and brought back to Jerusalem the War Scroll, the Thanksgiving Scroll (which he is shown examining in this photo) and the second of two Isaiah scrolls.

that I would reply to Lacheman's lecture and his contentions concerning the scrolls. I was flabbergasted. If I had had some warning, perhaps I could have prepared some more or less diplomatic words of disagreement. As it was, I gave an absolutely flat reply to Lacheman that what he had said was all nonsense. The scrolls were authentic documents of the pre-Christian period. Later, I spoke to Louise complaining that I should have been warned that I would be asked to speak. She knew Lacheman's views, a senior professor in the department, and my opposing views, a youngster just beginning his teaching. She replied, "I asked Ernest Lacheman to invite you to give a response to his lecture; I assumed that he had asked you." At the next department meeting, Louise dressed down Ernest Lacheman publicly. Alas, as a result, my relations with Lacheman were strained for the next 40 years; my attempts at reconciliation never really succeeded.

HS: Were your views on the dating of the scrolls based solely on paleography?

FMC: Initially, yes. But once the sectarian scrolls, especially the Commentary (*pešer*) on Habakkuk, the Rule of the Community and the War Scroll, were published, I began to have ideas about the origins of the scrolls on the basis of the content of the manuscripts, not only on the basis of the paleographical dates.

HS: What about the carbon 14 tests on the linen in which the scrolls were wrapped?

FMC: At that time carbon 14 dates were very crude. While the dates the tests gave were in broad agreement with the antiquity of the scrolls, they were not taken very seriously by anyone. Paleographical dating was more precise in the view of trained paleographers. Those arguing a late date for the scrolls simply ignored the carbon 14 data.

I approached the question of dating the scrolls first of all by the typology of the scripts used in the scrolls. Paleography in my opinion is still the most objective and precise means of dating the scrolls. Moreover, there is a scholarly consensus among trained paleographers about the scripts of this period. The new and more precise carbon 14 dates of the leather of the scrolls themselves, while further confirming the results of paleography (or vice versa), are still less reliable than paleography.

There is also typological dating of the jars and other artifacts found with the scrolls. With the excavation of Khirbet Qumrân, the archaeological sequencing of the artifacts found—including coins—and the paleographical dates of the scrolls formed parallel typologies in date. Within this framework established by paleography and archaeology, you can then move to the relatively subjective task of analyzing the historical allusions in the scrolls. Historical references in the scrolls of Cave 1 were veiled, written in the esoteric language of apocalyptic exegesis. Later, in Cave 4 documents, open references to figures of the Seleucid, Hasmonean and Roman periods were found.

The people whose lore is found in the sectarian scrolls—Essene scrolls I would call them—searched the Hebrew Bible for references to persons and events of their own time. They believed they lived in the last days, the end of days, and assumed biblical references to the future or to last times described their own time. All scripture was taken as prophetic, even the Psalms, and they looked for biblical sobriquets of persons that might fit their own time. In the biblical commentaries one finds references to a "Righteous Teacher" based on expressions found in Hosea 10:12 and Joel 2:23. They seized on this sobriquet and affixed it to their own priestly leader, probably the founder of the wilderness community at Qumrân. They found other sobriquets in scripture—the Wrathful Lion, the False Oracle, the Wicked Priest or Cursed Man.[2] They took these appellations and tagged them to figures of their own day and their own community. They expected two messiahs and found their titles in scripture, the "Star," the "Scepter" (from the Balaam oracles, Numbers 24:15-17), the "Son of God"[3] and so on. They believed these figures were about to appear in their midst, and in their ritual they enacted proleptically the Messianic Banquet of the End Time.

This kind of "eschatological exegesis" is also characteristic of the New Testament. An example is in the Gospel of John (1:19-23). Messengers sent to question John the Baptist ask him who he is. He replies that he is not the Messiah; he is not Elijah returned; he is not the (eschatological) prophet to come. Finally, he says of himself, "I am the voice of one crying in the wilderness, 'Make straight the way of the Lord...'" The biblical sobriquet John assumes is taken from

Isaiah 40:3. Like the sobriquet "Righteous Teacher," the original meaning of the phrase is reinterpreted by the eschatological exegete.

The veiled character of references to the chief figures of the sect—not known to history—and also to the important historical figures of the time makes the matter of reconstructing the history of the sect very difficult. Within the limits set by paleography and archaeology, there is some hope of success. If one ignores the limits of the more objective sciences—as some scholars still do—the task is hopeless, and possible identifications, if not endless, are many. Wicked priests are not a commodity in short supply.

HS: Between Lacheman's lecture at Wellesley and the time you were called to Jerusalem in 1953, what were your other contacts with the scrolls?

FMC: I wrote reviews of early studies of the scrolls, wrote briefly on the orthography (spelling) of the scrolls, and even tried my hand at some translation. The discussion and debate about the scrolls, their date and the community that owned them, as well as disputes concerning the character of the text of the Bible at Qumrân, came up at every scholarly meeting.

HS: What was the focus of the drama that was unfolding?

FMC: There were two foci in the scholarly discussions. One line of discussion was concerned with the history of the biblical text. The biblical scrolls from Qumrân were a millennium older than the manuscripts upon which the received text (the Masoretic text) was based. The biblical manuscripts from Cave 1 revealed a text of the Book of Isaiah that belonged to the main line of Palestinian tradition upon which the medieval biblical text of Isaiah was based. Still, the old Isaiah Scroll (1QIsa^a) exhibited variants in number and variety that differed *toto caelo* from any manuscript of the medieval era. Of particular interest was the orthography of the manuscript and readings held in common with the Old Greek (Septuagint) translation of the Book of Isaiah.

The discipline of textual criticism of the Hebrew Bible reached a nadir in the early part of this century. Most scholars more or less gave up trying to get behind the Rabbinic Recension of the first century C.E., from which all our medieval manuscripts stemmed. Many scholars had thought that the Pentateuch that survived in the Samaritan community provided a separate path to the pre-rabbinic text. But the Samaritan Pentateuch proved to be late and, indeed, influenced by the Rabbinic Recension of the Pentateuch.

The best avenue to the early Hebrew text was through the Old Greek translation of the Hebrew Bible, the so-called Septuagint, the oldest parts of which stemmed from the third century B.C.E. But Septuagint studies foundered in the first half of this century. Increasingly, conservative critics argued that apparent differences between the Greek translation and the traditional Hebrew rested not on different Hebrew texts being translated but upon the foibles of the Greek translators—their ignorance, their theological prejudices,

THE ABISHA SCROLL. A crazy quilt of patches characterizes the Abisha Scroll, the copy of the Pentateuch most revered by the Samaritans, a community that split off from mainstream Judaism sometime between the fourth century B.C.E. and the third century C.E. In the portion shown here, an unknown restorer has grafted the bottom portion of one column to the top of a second column; the widely spaced letters above the center of the newly formed column are characteristic of the bottoms of columns.

A cryptogram embedded in the scroll claims that it was written by Abisha, the great-grandson of the biblical Aaron, but scholars place the date of composition to the 12th century C.E. Professor Cross notes that the Samaritan version of the Pentateuch was heavily influenced by the Rabbinic Recension of the Hebrew Bible and is therefore less useful than the Septuagint for reconstructing pre-rabbinic versions of the Bible.

or their tendency for various reasons to gloss or abbreviate the text before them. The critical procedure of retroverting the Greek translation to the underlying Hebrew text, which in turn could be compared with the Hebrew of the Rabbinic Recension, was thus called into question. Was the Greek translator faithful to the Hebrew text he was translating? If not, the Old Greek translation was of no value for improving the Hebrew text or reconstructing its early history.

At the same time, many specialists in textual criticism began to question whether such an Old Greek translation had ever existed, or, if it had, if the "proto-Septuagint" could be reconstructed from extant Greek manuscripts of the Bible. A well known scholar named Paul Kahle argued that there was no proto-Septuagint, no single Old Greek translation, even of the Pentateuch; rather, Kahle claimed, many Greek translations were brought into conformity secondarily by recensional activities in the early Christian church. So, said Kahle, what we call the Septuagint was really a recension of a welter of Greek Targumim. All was chaos, and there was no reliable guide to the early Hebrew text.

If you have chaos and no reliable means to retrovert the Greek translation(s), you cannot attempt to reconstruct earlier readings in the text of the Bible. You cannot ferret out scribal errors or write the history of variant readings—the proper tasks of a textual critic. You can only resort to emendation in seeking the original text of the biblical author. The result is that the Masoretic text, or rather the Rabbinic Recension reconstructed from medieval Masoretic manuscripts, is left intact, uncriticized and authoritative. Textual criticism of the Hebrew Bible thus becomes not the search for more original forms of the text but the collation and evaluation of medieval Hebrew variants in an attempt to establish the precise text promulgated by the rabbis in the first century C.E. The era before the promulgation is left in the dark.

For many people, this is a comfortable state of affairs. The Masoretic text is canonical for both Jews and Protestants. The authoritative books of the Bible for Roman Catholics include the apocryphal books rejected in the Rabbinic Recension, but Jerome used the Masoretic text as the basis of his translation we now call the Vulgate. So readings of the traditional text are fixed. One doesn't have to worry about the foundational documents of faith and practice.

The trouble is that this approach is based on false premises. There *are* ways to get back to earlier stages of the biblical text and to improve readings in the text of the Hebrew Bible. This is the importance of the Qumrân biblical scrolls. Not only do they reflect more than one textual tradition in existence before the rabbinic text became authoritative, but they also furnish a host of variant readings. Some of the Qumrân manuscripts are closely related to the text used by the translators of the Old Greek Bible. They are important in demonstrating beyond cavil that the Jewish translators of the Greek Bible were normally faithful to the Hebrew manuscripts they were translating and that differences between the traditional text and the Old Greek text ordinarily reflect differences in *Hebrew* textual tradition, not the stupidities of the translators.

HS: You mentioned that the Masoretic text is canonical for Protestants. I thought the Protestant canon was based on the Septuagint, the Old Greek.

FMC: No. If you read the confessions of the Protestant Reformation, you will find that, as far as the "Old Testament" is concerned, the Hebrew (Masoretic) text and canon are declared the only authoritative basis for faith and practice. Luther's famous translation of the Old Testament was from the Masoretic text, and he loudly urged young theologians to learn Hebrew to enable themselves to exegete Scripture properly. Calvin was a Hebrew scholar, and his commentaries are based on the Masoretic text. The Roman Catholic Church at the Council of Trent during the Counter-Reformation declared a broader canon (as well as church tradition) authoritative, including the apocryphal books preserved largely in Greek and, explicitly, the text of Jerome's Vulgate. However, as I noted earlier, the Vulgate translation of Jerome was regularly based on the Hebrew Bible in books extant in the Masoretic text, and Jerome explicitly rejected the Greek version underlying the Old Latin translation in favor of the "Hebraica veritas."

HS: Is the Revised Standard Version of the Old Testament, for example, based on the Masoretic text?

FMC: Yes. Let me return to our discussion of the impact of the Qumrân scrolls on textual criticism of the Hebrew Bible. When the biblical texts from Qumrân and other sites in the Jordan Rift are fully published, we will be able to study and evaluate a multitude of variant readings, that is, readings that vary from the traditional text. In many ways more important, we will know better how to use the Old Greek translation and its variants. Controls we did not possess before will be at hand. The history of the Greek text has been vividly illuminated. We now have new ways to get back to the proto-Septuagint. The stages of its history are revealed, as well as the origins of the later recensions and later Greek revisions of the Old Greek. Kahle's theory of Greek Targumim is refuted, particularly on the basis of evidence from *Greek* manuscripts from Qumrân and the southern desert, notably the Greek Minor Prophets Scroll from the Naḥal Ḥever. In short, these discoveries lead us along a path that goes behind the barrier of the Rabbinic Recension and the stabilization of the Hebrew text.

HS: We were talking about the excitement over the scrolls before you left to begin work in Jerusalem. You mentioned two foci of excitement. One was new resources for the history of the text of the Hebrew Bible. What was the other one?

FMC: The other was the light the scrolls shed on the religious currents in Judaism in the period immediately before the establishment of rabbinic orthodoxy and immediately before the crystallization of Christian orthodoxy.

There is no hint of any Christian material in the scrolls—despite what one may read in the press. The scrolls are Jewish documents. So far as I know, there are no references to Christianity or to Christian figures in the scrolls. However, the scrolls and the religious literature they contain stem from the time and place that Christianity was coming to birth. If the library of Qumrân furnishes us a new window on the last 200 years before the destruction of the Second Temple by Rome, it teaches us not only an immense amount about the history of Judaism, but also about the history of early (Jewish) Christianity. If you can place hitherto isolated facts, issues, institutions, polemics, language, beliefs and hopes found in the earliest Christian literature into their proper Jewish historical background where there is a similar or identical social and religious environment, you gain a much richer and nuanced understanding of early

Christianity. Equally important, the sectarian literature of this period presents us with a new picture of a rich and complex Judaism in the period before the total dominance of the House of Hillel.

HS: Rabbinic Judaism?

FMC: Yes, rabbinic Judaism. Before the ascendancy of the Pharisees and the emergence of rabbinic orthodoxy after the fall of the Second Temple, Judaism was more complex and variegated than we had supposed. The apocalyptic strain in Judaism was much stronger and more widespread than historians of Judaism have thought. Literature with strains of apocalyptic eschatology and exegesis found in such works as Daniel and Revelation, and particularly in the Pseudepigrapha, should have given us warning. But such literature was considered peripheral, the product of strange dreamers on the fringes of Judaism, not the doctrine of major Jewish communities or sects. George Foot Moore in his monumental three-volume work on Judaism speaks of the apocalyptic literature like this: "[I]nasmuch as these writings have never been recognized by Judaism, it is a fallacy of method for the historian to make them a primary source for the eschatology of Judaism, much more to contaminate its theology with them."[4]

HS: We should also have known the importance of the apocalyptic movement from the New Testament.

FMC: Yes, we should have. Since Albert Schweitzer's revolutionary attempt to use the literature of the apocalyptic movement and its "thoroughgoing eschatology" as a basis for understanding the historical Jesus and Paul, the pertinence of this literature for Christian origins has been clear. Schweitzer put it bluntly: "Jesus was the high-water mark of Jewish Apocalypticism."[5] My colleague Helmut Koester has written—in the full light of the new discoveries—"The apocalyptic movement became the most important theological movement in Judaism during the Hellenistic period, and it was also to play a decisive role in the formation of Christianity."[6]

But many scholars, both Jewish and Christian, prefer to downplay apocalyptic elements in their traditions. Not surprisingly, the apocalyptic elements in the New Testament are awkward or distasteful to many Christian theologians and apologists. If they cannot rid the early church of apocalypticism, they can at least claim that Jesus himself and his authentic words were free of this sort of nonsense. The fact is, however, that Jesus lived and died in a world of apocalyptic fervor. If he is fully freed from this world, he ceases to be a historical figure.

HS: It is interesting that the Dead Sea Scrolls illuminate a whole complex of issues that are also in other old sources but which we really did not understand fully.

FMC: Yes. An example may be found in the document with the unhappy title of MMT *(Miqṣê ma'ăśê hat-tôrâ)*—which I prefer to designate the "Halakhic Epistle [or Letter]." It is a public letter debating halakhic issues, that is, matters of religious law, especially questions of ritual purity. In many cases the positions taken can now be seen as halakhic positions the Pharisees opposed in Talmudic discourse and that can be assigned to Zadokite (Sadducean) legal tradition.

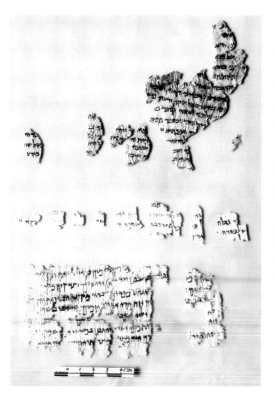

MMT. The inelegant title of this document is a Hebrew acronym, but Professor Cross prefers to call it the "Halakhic Epistle," or letter on Jewish law. No complete text of MMT has been found, but the document was partially reconstructed from six incomplete manuscripts by Elisha Qimron, an Israeli scholar, and John Strugnell. The roughly 120 lines of MMT that have been reconstructed contain calendrical material and a list of more than 20 rules on ritual purity, issues over which the Qumrân sect broke with the priests of the Jerusalem Temple. In many instances the positions espoused by MMT match those of the Sadducees as recorded in the Talmud.

HS: But they don't seem to be debating apocalyptic issues in this halakhic epistle.

FMC: No, this is true. But it does not mean the letter was not written by a member or members of a community, the Essene community I believe, that belonged to the apocalyptic movement. In the sectarian documents at Qumrân, radically conservative concerns with legal lore are combined with descriptions of the New Age of redemption, and, as I have mentioned, the Messianic Banquet was proleptically realized in their rituals.

To be sure, there has been a strong element of scholarship, especially under the influence of German form-critical doctrine, that has transferred categories used in searching for layers of tradition and the separation of documents (oral or written) in biblical studies to the sectarian Qumrân literature. In particular, there are distinctions between proclamation and law, prophetic tradition and legal tradition, kerygma and didache, dogma and ethics. These genres are rooted finally in the sharp separation of law and grace common to radical Pauline or Lutheran theology, and they have philosophic support in German academic idealism.

Past analysis of the so-called Damascus Document is a case in point. The early sections of the Damascus Document review the history of God's mighty acts down to the rise of the sect, quoting scriptural texts predicting these events of the last times. It is typical of the preaching and exegesis we associate with the apocalyptic movement. The last sections of the Damascus Document are concerned with covenant law and the exposition of the legal discipline of the sect. Before the discovery of the copies of the Damascus Document at Qumrân, the two sections of the Damascus Document were declared to be two different works copied together by chance. Now the two sections appear combined in the copies from Qumrân Cave 4.

This has led not to acceptance of the document as a single work but to new efforts to find underlying written sources, some more or less legal (and early), others more or less characterized by apocalyptic eschatology (and thus later). Some of the legal and "kerygmatic" elements in this and other works may have had independent existence. The same biblical proof texts with the same bizarre interpretations appear in different sectarian works, some stemming no doubt from *testimonia* lists (collections of biblical proof texts). And no doubt some of the rules of community life existed in writing and in oral lore before they were set down in various forms in the several sectarian works that systematize the legal tradition at Qumrân. But the point is that an intense interest in halakhic issues combined with an intense preoccupation with apocalyptic beliefs and speculations characterize the community. The Damascus Document is a single composition from early in the community's life, which continued to be copied late.

As early as 1960, Klaus Baltzer, in an important study called *Das Bundesformular* (published in English as *The Covenant Formulary*), showed that the Damascus Document followed an old traditional pattern or genre, which he called the "covenant formulary."[7] The pattern appears and reappears in the Hebrew Bible, in sectarian Jewish texts and indeed in early Christian literature. The juxtaposition of the dogmatic and legal sections should have been seen by scholars as an argument for the unity of the work.

HS: So Qumrân tradition really reflects rather the combination of the two.

FMC: Yes, it seems so to me.

HS: How did you get involved officially with the scrolls?

FMC: What actually sent me to the scrollery in Jerusalem to begin work on the manuscripts themselves was the discovery of Cave 4 in 1952.

HS: Cave 4 was the mother lode. It is adjacent to the settlement that scholars were excavating, and yet they didn't find it. The bedouin found Cave 4 and excavated most of it.

FMC: Yes, the earlier scholarly expedition that searched the caves looked up in the rocky cliffs above the marl terrace. This was where the bedouin shepherds had found Cave 1 and indeed where Cave 2 (found by bedouin), Cave 3 (found by scholars) and Cave 11 (found by bedouin) were situated. These were natural caves, and the high cliffs were honeycombed with them.

THE DAMASCUS DOCU-MENT. Twice buried, twice uncovered, this 10th-century C.E. manuscript, now known as the Damascus Document, provided the first glimpse of an ancient Jewish sect. Discovered in 1897 in the *genizah* of a Cairo synagogue by the Jewish scholar Solomon Schechter, this text (left) contains a furious condemnation of the ritual practices of opponents of the sect. On the basis of the language and ideas in the text, Schechter concluded that this document was a medieval version of a much earlier text. The discovery of the Dead Sea Scrolls half a century later proved him right. Among the scrolls were ancient copies of Schechter's document.

Professor Cross notes that scholars have long been puzzled by the seemingly implausible combination of legal arcana and apocalyptic speculation in the Damascus Document; some have even suggested that the legal and apocalyptic sections of the text were composed separately and combined later. Cross argues that the Damascus Document follows a classic pattern in Jewish literature in which apocalyptic concerns and legal issues are combined in a single work. He therefore believes that the Damascus Document is a uniform work that was composed early in the life of the Qumrân community and was frequently copied thereafter.

HS: Why the hell didn't you look in the marl terrace?

FMC: Don't look at me. I was not with the teams of explorers. I came to Jerusalem after Cave 4 was discovered. I guess the leaders of the scholarly expedition that searched for caves thought that, given limited time and money, their best chance of finding more scrolls was in the kind of terrain and type of cave where previous finds had been made. Had I been on the team of exploration, I probably would have reasoned, alas, as they did. The bedouin were brighter and more flexible. Incidentally, Cave 4 was originally an Iron Age tomb.

HS: How do you know that?

FMC: The shape and floor plan of the tomb together with the fact that natural caves are not found in marl of this sort. Several of the cave-tombs in the marl terrace originally belonged to the small, seventh-century B.C.E. village at Qumrân that underlay the Hellenistic-Roman ruin. The people of the village, probably one of the biblical towns in the desert province listed in Joshua 15, dug typical Iron Age tombs. These were later reused by people of the sect, the Essenes, just as they used some of the natural rocky caves high in the cliffs.

FRANK MOORE CROSS, dapper but serious, stands at the entrance to Cave 1 at Qumrân. In 1953 Cross was appointed by the American Schools of Oriental Research to an international team of scholars to publish the scroll fragments found the previous year in Cave 4. Cross subsequently assumed a professorship at Harvard, but has continued his work on Cave 4 materials as well as on papyrus fragments found at Wâdī ed-Dâliyeh, north of Jericho.

They lived in some of these old tombs (as they did in the natural caves), and, in at least one instance, they dumped the remains of their library in a tomb (Cave 4).

Incidentally, bedouin and later scholars did not walk into these reused tombs and find the floors littered with manuscript fragments. Discovery of the manuscripts was not just a matter of peering into an opening in the marl terrace. The fragments were excavated first by the bedouin and then, at the deepest levels, by scholars. Over the long centuries, the floor of the tomb had filled slowly with roof fall, with accretions of wind-blown dust and with the droppings of animals. The floors and ceilings of caves, especially caves in soft marl, tend to move upwards.

HS: The floor moves up?

FMC: Yes, it rises with the accumulation of the centuries. The ceiling moves upwards owing to roof falls and erosion from wind-blown sand. Several of the tombs had collapsed in antiquity. The Taʿâmireh tribesmen knew enough to excavate the floors of caves. These same Taʿâmireh, or rather their fathers, had been workmen for anthropologists in the excavation of prehistoric caves in the sides of canyons of the Jordan Rift. So the excavation of caves was a professional endeavor (laughter) on their part. They knew to look in dry caves, and they knew that patient excavation was required to recover artifacts. In Cave 4, they made their greatest find, and they had almost completed the excavation of the cave before they were halted by the Department of Antiquities.

HS: It was about 80 percent empty by the time the archaeologists found it?

FMC: At least 80 percent. I should say over 90 percent. Still, fragments of 25 or more manuscripts were excavated by archaeologists led by Roland de Vaux. I worked on the excavated lot throughout the summer of 1953 before they were joined in the fall with two large lots purchased from the middleman of the Taʿâmireh. Purchases of Cave 4 lots continued for another five years, until 1958.

QUMRÂN CAVE 4, called the mother lode, is seen at center in this photo. The cave—originally an Iron Age tomb—lies within the marl terrace just below the Qumrân settlement on the plateau above. The cave was the repository of the largest number of manuscript fragments found in any single cave—15,000, from nearly 600 documents.

Ironically, Cave 4 was not discovered by the scholars excavating the settlement and exploring the cliffs above, but by bedouin shepherds. By the time scholars discovered the bedouin at work, they had unearthed nearly all the manuscript fragments. The archaeological community in east Jerusalem, then in Jordanian hands, arranged to purchase the tens of thousands of fragments from the bedouin. A small team of scholars from several national schools of research was appointed to edit and publish them.

INTERIOR OF CAVE 4. The spic-and-span condition of the interior of Cave 4 today belies the conditions in which the bedouin (and later, scholars) worked to recover the thousands of fragments, which were buried under more than 6 feet of bat dung, windblown dust and roof fall that had accumulated over the centuries.

HS: These fellows (the Ta'âmireh bedouin) were going in and out of Cave 4 digging away while Khirbet Qumrân was being excavated by archaeologists?

FMC: As far as I know, not while the archaeologists were actually digging the *khirbeh*. They dug for Roland de Vaux and Lankester Harding on the tell when it was being excavated. They dug for themselves only when the Western scholars retired to Jerusalem.

HS: The Qumrân site is not a tell, is it?

FMC: I guess you can call it a small tell. To be precise, it is a *khirbeh*, an ancient ruin. It does, however, consist of a number of layers or strata, as does a true tell, with its sequence of destroyed cities, debris forming a truncated cone.

In any case, Cave 4 was found and dug initially by the indefatigable Ta'âmireh. It was a remarkable find, indeed a unique find, both in the enormous quantity of manuscript remains it produced and in the fragmentary character of the contents. To cope with a discovery of that size, the archaeological community in Jerusalem organized itself to raise funds and appointed a team of scholars to work on the material. Leadership in this endeavor was taken by the Palestine Archaeological Museum as it was then called, the Rockefeller Museum as it is called today.

Until it was nationalized in 1966, the Rockefeller was a private museum, with a curiously composed board. The trustees were drawn, one each, from the national schools of biblical and archaeological research in Jerusalem. A group of lay trustees, diplomats from the countries with national schools of research in Jerusalem, completed the board. Thus the director of the American School of Oriental Research and the American ambassador, or the American consul in Jerusalem, were the American representatives on the board. Similarly, the British School of Archaeology had two representatives. The French school, the École Biblique et Archéologique Française, had two representatives, one of whom, Roland de Vaux, was president of the board in the 1950s. Finally, the Jewish Exploration Society as it was known before 1948, later the Israel Exploration Society, had two positions *de jure,* or by tradition, on the board. The curator of the museum served as secretary to the board. I believe this was all. Other national schools, more recent institutions, were not added to the board as far as I know.

HS: You are describing the makeup of the board before 1948?

FMC: Yes. After 1948 the representatives of the Israel Exploration Society were unable to attend. Jordan, which exercised rule over old Jerusalem where the museum was situated, and Israel were in a state of war.

THE QUMRÂN SETTLEMENT, shown here from the northeast, measures about 240 feet east to west and 325 feet north to south. Caves 4 and 5 appear to the left of center. Originally inhabited in the eighth to early sixth centuries B.C.E., Qumrân was resettled sometime during the reign of John Hyrcanus (134-104 B.C.E.) by the sect that produced the Dead Sea Scrolls. Earthquake and fire destroyed the site in 31 B.C.E., but it was later rebuilt. This phase of habitation lasted until 68 C.E., when the settlement was sacked during the Roman suppression of the First Jewish Revolt. Qumrân then became a small Roman outpost, which was abandoned after the Romans overran the last Jewish stronghold at Masada in 73 or 74 C.E. For the next 1,900 years, this obscure desert enclave lay mostly covered, until the chance discovery of the Dead Sea Scrolls focused international attention on the site.

HS: Were the Israelis still on the board?

FMC: I don't know. There were slots on the board for the Jewish representatives. Whether they were appointed and whether there was communication with them, I do not know. I was a member of the board only in 1953 when I first went to Jerusalem. I was acting director of the American School for part of the year, and as such actually attended a meeting of the Board of Trustees of the museum. At any rate, the trustees of the museum determined to ask each school represented on the board to nominate scholars for the team to edit the manuscripts of Cave 4. Funds to support the team, and for additional purchases of Cave 4 fragments dug by bedouin, were also solicited from these schools as well as from other scholarly institutions in the West.

I was nominated by the American Schools of Oriental Research and, as it happened, was the first of the Cave 4 team to arrive in Jerusalem, in early June 1953. I went to Jerusalem wearing two hats. I was also to be annual professor at the American School. That post actually supported me and my family for the year. It was when I arrived in Jerusalem and settled in at the American School that I first met Père de Vaux. He came over to the school and conducted me to the museum, to the scrollery. I met (G. Lankester) Harding at the same time. He was curator of the Palestine Archaeological Museum

PÈRE ROLAND DE VAUX "wore his Dominican robes with great flair," Cross says of the monk, distinguished biblical scholar and archaeologist. De Vaux led the excavation team at Qumrân and the scroll scholars assigned to publish the Cave 4 fragments. He wrote annual reports of the dig until his death in 1971 and published a book of lectures on the site. The final excavation report is now being prepared by Robert Donceel and Pauline Donceel-Voûte of Fribourg University (Switzerland) and Louvain University (Belgium) in conjunction with Jean Batiste Humbert of the École Biblique in Jerusalem.

as well as the director of antiquities of Jordan, one of the last of a breed of Englishmen who held high posts in the government of Jordan. Harding holding these two posts was fortunate for the future of scroll studies. As director of antiquities, he maintained the special diplomatic status of the West Bank, assigning all of the scrolls found on the West Bank to the (private) Rockefeller Museum of which he was curator. He saw the wisdom of not separating the material and of having the team appointed by the museum board.

HS: Who made the deal with the bedouin to buy the scroll fragments for one dinar per square centimeter of inscribed surface?

FMC: Basically, this arrangement, which gave Kando (Khalil Iskander Shahin, a Syrian Christian antiquities dealer) *de facto* immunity from

G. LANKESTER HARDING (right), head of the Jordanian Department of Antiquities, Roland de Vaux (left) and Jozef Milik, a scrolls editor, examine a small jug from Qumrân. Harding, a reserved Englishman, was the opposite of the gregarious de Vaux in personality. Like many Englishmen of his generation, Harding fell in love with Arab culture and lived as an Arab. When Jordanian nationalists finally ousted him from his post, he retired to a small Arab village. Harding outlasted all of his English colleagues as an employee of Jordan.

the antiquities laws, so long as he brought all scroll fragments in his control directly to the museum for purchase at a standard price, was de Vaux's doing rather than Harding's. Harding and de Vaux obviously worked hand in hand. The arrangement could not work unless Harding, whose task was to enforce the antiquities laws, silently acquiesced. But he could not negotiate directly with Kando. Increasingly, too, Harding deferred to de Vaux, for whom he had enormous respect, in all matters relating to the scrolls.

HS: Tell me a little bit about their personalities.

FMC: De Vaux was a distinguished scholar, the dominant figure in archaeological and biblical studies residing in the Arab sector of Jerusalem. He was a leading liberal figure in Catholic biblical studies although he looked middle-of-the-road or conservative to Protestant biblical scholars. He was a major figure in the effort to open the Bible to Catholic laymen and a pioneer among Catholic scholars in the critical study of the Bible. Personally, he was completely charming—brilliant, lively and warm. He wore his Dominican robes with great flair. He was a raconteur of extraordinary gifts.

HS: They say he was once a member of the Comédie Française.

FMC: That tale circulated widely in his lifetime. If you had known him, you would understand why. He had wit and a gift for the dramatic. I once asked him if the story of his acting career were true. He laughed and said no. He was brought up to be a pious lad destined to join the Dominican order. But he was obviously delighted with the story. I came to know him well when he came to Harvard for a year as a visiting professor. He was a delightful and amiable colleague.

Harding could not have contrasted more in personality. He was a fairly shy man, a little gruff, with a great deal of English reserve. Harding was one of a number of Englishmen who found acceptance in the Near East they could not find at home, and he fell in love with Arab culture. He began work as an archaeologist but became increasingly interested in early Arabic inscriptions. He was completely fluent in Arabic. He lived as an Arab; and when he was finally thrown out of office by Jordanian nationalists, he retired to a small Arab village in Lebanon.

I think Harding was the last of the British civil servants in the employ of Jordan. Glubb Pasha lasted a surprisingly long time as head of the Arab Legion, but Harding survived even longer.

HS: What happened to Lankester Harding?

FMC: He died in Lebanon. He survived de Vaux who died at the relatively young age of 67 in 1971. When I arrived in 1953, Harding and de Vaux suggested that I begin by preparing and identifying manuscript fragments that had been excavated by their expedition after illicit digging by Taʿâmireh had been halted.

HS: You didn't have the material the bedouin had excavated in Cave 4 yet?

FMC: No, but a great deal had been bought. After the resources of the museum had been exhausted, Harding prevailed on the Jordanian government to make a grant of 15,000 dinars (equivalent to £15,000) to purchase the first two lots of fragments in bedouin hands. Purchases by various foreign institutions were yet to be organized. However, it was decided that it would be useful for me to attack the fragments of certain provenience and to await the coming of other members of the team of editors before bringing out the very large purchased lots, which were stored in the museum safe.

HS: Did you have anything to do with the excavation?

FMC: No, not with the excavation of the cave; that was before I arrived in Jerusalem.

HS: So you had to work initially without 80 percent or more of the Cave 4 material.

FMC: Yes. However, I had a small cross section of what turned up in the large lots of purchased fragments. The overlap was useful for proving the provenience of the purchased lots. That summer I read many of the documents that have now become famous, including a piece of the Halakhic Letter (MMT), which because of its special dialect I labeled in my notes the "proto-Mishnaic" document.

The most excitement I had that summer in the scrollery came when I prepared some unsavory, dark fragments found deep in a hole in the floor of Cave 4. The fragments were encrusted with yellow crystals that appeared to be dried urine. The encrustation completely obscured the writing on the surface of the leather. I used castor oil, reputedly the most stable of oils, and a camel-hair brush to try to clean the surface enough to read it. Gradually, little bits of the script became legible. I could see enough to conclude that the manuscript was about Samuel and that Samuel was a Nazirite. There were enough differences from the Masoretic text of Samuel that I concluded that it was not a biblical manuscript, and I put it aside as a story about Samuel, perhaps an apocryphon. Then I went on to other things. Wherever I turned there was excitement.

In the course of studying some biblical texts, notably an old copy of Exodus, I was using a Hebrew Bible and also a copy of the Greek Bible, the *Larger Cambridge Septuagint*, comparing variant readings, when it occurred to me that I should check the Greek text of Samuel (which is very different from the Masoretic text) to see if the Greek text had any of the readings I had found in the encrusted manuscript I had been cleaning. I immediately found one or two and resumed cleaning the fragments feverishly—which amounted finally to some 25 in number in the excavated lot, part of two adjacent columns. The manuscript continued to produce readings in common with the Old Greek translation of Samuel.

I suddenly realized I had found something that to me and to other textual critics of the Hebrew Bible was earthshaking. My manuscript of Samuel was related to the Hebrew manuscript of Samuel used by Jewish translators of the Hebrew Bible into Greek. It proved that the translator of the Old Greek had been faithful to the Hebrew text he was translating. Thus the differences between the traditional Hebrew text and the Old Greek translation, for the most part, rested on different textual traditions of the Hebrew Bible. The manuscript of Samuel promised to break the logjam in text-critical studies of the Hebrew Bible. I held a key discovery.

HS: Right in your hand?

FMC: Yes, this little group of fragments could be held in my hand. But their significance was enormous and clear. I hurriedly completed cleaning and patching together the fragments and prepared an article to announce the discovery and publish the text. I sent it to the *Bulletin of the American Schools of Oriental Research* for the issue honoring C. C. Torrey. It appeared under the title "A New Qumran Biblical Fragment Related to the Original Hebrew Underlying the Septuagint."[8] The manuscript was labeled 4QSam[a], a siglum we have kept, though earlier exemplars of Samuel have turned up in the purchased lots. More of this manuscript, 4QSam[a], was found in the purchased lots, as we discovered later, and now it is the most extensively preserved biblical manuscript from Cave 4 and certainly the most important.

HS: Were you all alone that summer?

FMC: Yes, no one was working in the scrollery but me. J. T. Milik, a Pole appointed as a French team member who had worked earlier on fragments from Cave 1, arrived in the fall of 1953. With his arrival, we brought out the lots of scroll fragments purchased to that date from the bedouin. A grant came from John D. Rockefeller, Jr., through the agency of Carl Kraeling of the American Schools, to underwrite the expenses of the team and of a permanent photographer. John Allegro, representing the British School, arrived in late autumn 1953. In 1954, Jean Starcky, John Strugnell, Patrick Skehan and Claus-Hunno Hunzinger were added to the team.

HS: Joseph Fitzmyer recalls that the last item purchased was what we now call 4Q246, the Son of God text.

FMC: Yes, it was one of the documents in the last purchases. The last purchases were made in 1958. I was involved in one purchase in 1956, thanks to the benefaction of a donor to McCormick Theological Seminary in Chicago, and two purchases in 1958, one made possible by a second gift from the donor to the McCormick Theological Seminary, the other by a gift from the All Souls Unitarian Church in New York City. A gift came, too, from Oxford University in 1958, and I believe it was in their lot that the Son of

THE FRAGMENT KNOWN AS 4QSamᵃ was found in a deep hole in the floor of Cave 4. When Cross first examined it, the letters were almost completely obscured by a yellow encrustation apparently of dried animal urine. Using a camel-hair brush and castor oil, Cross managed to render the fragment partially legible. He recognized that the text was about Samuel, but because the passage differed from the Masoretic text, he put it aside thinking it was an apocryphal version of the biblical book.

When he later compared this version to the text of Samuel in the Septuagint, the third- to second-century B.C.E. Greek translation of the Hebrew Bible that varies from the traditional text, he suddenly realized he was holding a fragment of earth-shattering significance to textual scholars of the Bible. The Hebrew version of Samuel preserved in the Cave 4 fragment was from the text on which the Septuagint translation was based. Up to that time, scholars had thought that differences between the Septuagint and the Masoretic text were the fault of careless scribes. Cross had deciphered the first evidence of a non-Masoretic Hebrew text of the Bible.

God text was recovered—part of the extracanonical Daniel literature. I must confess, however, that I was under the impression that the All Souls Deuteronomy was the last manuscript recovered from Cave 4; but perhaps Fitzmyer is correct, and the All Souls purchase was merely the last purchase in which I was personally involved—that is the last purchase before the discovery of Cave 11, when I again negotiated on behalf of the American Schools.

HS: The high point of your summer was the discovery of the Cave 4 Samuel?

FMC: Yes, no doubt. There is a follow-up story. In the early fall, my old teacher, Albright, came to Jerusalem. He was a guest of the Israelis but was determined to make the "reverse crossing" from Israeli Jerusalem into the Old City controlled by Jordan to see old Père Hughes Vincent at the Dominican convent and, incidentally, to visit me in the scrollery. Vincent was a lifelong friend of his. Albright's eldest son, Hugh, was named after Vincent. Furthermore, it was Vincent who was responsible for Albright's wife, Ruth, converting to Catholicism. After threatening to divorce his wife (Albright grew up in South America, the son of a Methodist missionary to Roman Catholics), Albright entered into personal and scholarly discourse with Vincent. Albright was disarmed—and charmed, and a remarkable friendship ensued.

At the time Albright visited Jerusalem in 1953, Vincent was in his nineties, I believe, and both men knew it would be their last meeting. I accompanied Albright to the Dominican convent and witnessed their meeting and embrace. They spoke French together. Both men were weeping. So I quickly withdrew and waited for Albright in the garden. When Albright came out, I took him (trailed by an escort of secret police accorded everyone who made the reverse crossing) over to the scrollery in the museum. I showed him the Samuel fragments and a draft of my paper listing the readings and my evaluations of them. From that day forward, Albright completely changed the approach to the Masoretic text he had followed for most of his life.

HS: What was the change?

FMC: Up to then, he had been very chary of making changes in the Masoretic text. Only if the text made no apparent sense would he tamper with it. And even then he preferred to play with the *matres lectionis* (late elements in the texts, the consonants *w*, *y* and *h* used as markers for vowels) in order to change the text or the meaning of a word or to look for emendations that had graphic similarity to the Masoretic consonantal text. He was not a Masoretic fundamentalist, but he rarely made full use of the versions in establishing the biblical text. From 1953 on, he took the witness of the Greek text very seriously; indeed, I became alarmed that, with the zeal of a convert, he sometimes made uncritical use of the Old Greek translation.

I was raised in the text-critical school represented by Albright and most other scholars of the first half of the century. Confrontation with the biblical scrolls from the Judean desert forced me to develop new theories and approaches to comprehend the new data. Many other students of Albright still follow the "early Albright" in text-critical methodology. Change is difficult, and the older a scholar is the more difficult it usually is for him to make fundamental changes in his methods and practice. Albright changed his views in the space of an afternoon of study of 4QSam^a. I think this is a mark of greatness. Whenever new evidence came to light, Albright rearranged his intellectual furnishings to bring the new into a synthesis with the old. He was criticized for changing his mind so often. However, he rarely changed his position unless there were new data; and when there were new data that required him to abandon old positions, he did so with alacrity.

I know many scholars who spend their aging years defending their earlier views against the ravages of new evidence and new discussions, a pitiful perversion of scholarship, more defensive of the self than of the truth. I think that being an archaeologist may have helped Albright maintain flexibility. In archaeology, there is constant change and a constant supply of new data. One must change to survive. Biblical scholars tend to be more rigid than archaeologists, more stubborn about giving up antiquated views—perhaps because the literary sciences are so much softer than the typological and technical sciences that dominate archaeology.

HS: What was it like to purchase scrolls from the bedouin?

FMC: As I have said, I was involved in a series of purchases. The acquisition of the last lots of the Cave 4 materials was interesting. The best fragments, best in size and preservation, were saved until last. The All Souls Deuteronomy is a large, handsome piece of leather. The pseudo-Daniel piece with the hymn concerning the "son of God" appeared late, with most of a column well preserved. A large, legible fragment of the old Samuel scroll, 4QSam^b, a scroll dating to the mid-third century B.C.E., came in one of the last lots. It was a beautiful piece, which was on display in the museum. Alas, it disappeared during the Six-Day War in 1967.

HS: I wonder if it will ever surface?

FMC: I think it may turn up; obviously, I very much hope it will find its way back to the museum. I should say that we know of a number of fragments that are in private hands. Diplomats and collectors acquired them and smuggled them out of the country. They were purchased from Kando or other antiquities dealers acting as middlemen for the bedouin. Even with his immunity agreement, Kando did not have a total monopoly, particularly in the early years.

HS: Sukenik's purchase of three intact scrolls from Cave 1 didn't come from Kando.

FMC: No, they did not. The primary figure in that negotiation was Levon Ohan, an Armenian antiquities dealer in the Old City, the son

WILLIAM FOXWELL ALBRIGHT, a giant of American biblical studies and archaeology, became a mentor to Cross at Johns Hopkins. While Albright was visiting Jerusalem in 1953, Cross showed him the 4QSam^a fragment, and Albright instantly changed his lifelong approach to problems in the Masoretic text. Previously he had restricted himself to emending the Hebrew text almost solely to changes that were graphically similar to the consonantal Masoretic text.

of the old Ohan, the most famous antiquities dealer during the British mandate. Ohan *fils* was never mentioned in Sukenik's accounts. Presumably Sukenik was trying to protect him. But it was Ohan who went back and forth to Bethlehem dickering for the scrolls.

Kando finally gained a monopoly or near monopoly on the new finds by becoming the business partner of the sheikh of the Ta'âmireh and by establishing and following the arrangement that gave him immunity from criminal arrest as long as he sold to the museum. Before that he had been harassed by the police for breach of the antiquities laws and had taken various measures to conceal the fragments. One bushel basket of scroll material was buried in Bethlehem, if we can believe Kando's story, and when it was dug up after the hill country winter, the leather had turned to glue.

HS: Kando never told the story of his involvement with the scrolls.

FMC: There were attempts to record his memoirs, but he always refused. Now he is dead, and we shall never know his story. If he had recounted his part in the history of the scrolls, I doubt if any of us would have been able to distinguish between what was true and what was false. He was a canny and attractive rogue and a gifted liar. I sometimes wondered if *he* knew when he was lying and when he was merely ornamenting the truth.

HS: Can you describe a purchase?

KHALIL ISKANDER SHAHIN (Kando), a cobbler and antiquities dealer, is described by Cross as "a canny and attractive rogue and a gifted liar." Kando played the role of middleman between the bedouin and scholars in negotiations for the Cave 4 fragments. The parties had agreed on a price of one Jordanian dinar (about $2.80 at the time) for each square centimeter of inscribed leather. Kando, however, claimed an additional fee for large or elegant pieces. Despite Kando's wrangling ever higher prices from the scholars, Cross feels that, in the light of history, the scholars were the clear winners.

FMC: I remember my first purchase. In the summer of 1956, I advised de Vaux and Harding that I had the first of two gifts from McCormick Theological Seminary, a sum of $6,000. Word was sent to Kando, probably by Yusuf Saʿad, the secretary of the museum. Kando was told that 2,100 square centimeters of inscribed leather from Cave 4 would be paid for if he brought the material to the Palestine Archaeological Museum. At 10 a.m. the next morning he appeared at the museum. We met in the inner garden of the museum with its lovely reflecting pool lined about with lavender. We drank coffee and attempted conversation for about ten minutes. Saʿad, who was equally fluent in Arabic, French and English, was our interpreter. Niceties completed, we got down to bargaining.

Kando stuck to the agreement of one Jordanian dinar (about $2.80 at that time) for each square centimeter of inscribed material—but claimed a *baksheesh* for particularly large or elegant pieces. The bargaining was really over the large pieces. These last finds had many large pieces, and the $2.80 figure rarely applied, at least in Kando's mind. We acquired the handsome lot, and before Kando could get to the bank, we were busy identifying the new fragments and joining them to our manuscripts in the scrollery.

One other tale. Cave 11 was discovered in the early spring of 1956. In 1960, on behalf of the American Schools of Oriental Research, I negotiated the purchase of the so-called Psalms Scroll from Cave 11, the document later edited by J. A. Sanders. A large purchase price was made available by a gift of the late Elizabeth Bechtel. The former price of $2.80 per square centimeter was not even the basis for negotiation on this major scroll. We negotiated at great length without success. Kando was wily and, although unlettered, knew the worth of his goods. I finally threw up my hands. I said, I have this check; it is all I have. Take it or leave it. I put the check on the table. Kando stuck out his hand to seal the bargain grinning from ear to ear.

HS: How much was it?

FMC: Sixty thousand dollars. Kando asked to accompany me to the bank, the Arab Bank under the arches across from the Damascus Gate, where the check had to be changed into cash. I had no objection. When I got there with Kando, I noticed a number of Taʿâmireh tribesmen standing about. We were being carefully watched. I went into the bank and got a paper sack full of money. Kando watched to see that every bill they gave me for the check went into the bag. I gave him the bag once we got outside the bank. Kando watched me, and the bedouin watched us both.

After 1967 I learned, to my dismay, that Yusuf Saʿad, who had done all my bargaining through the years, was a silent partner of Kando's. [Laughter] I am sure Kando knew the amount written on my cashier's check as well as I did. A Westerner never wins in the oriental bazaar. And yet I must say that in reality we won every time.

HS: In a historical light, you did.

THE PALESTINE ARCHAEOLOGICAL MUSEUM. Completed in 1938 with a grant from John D. Rockefeller, Jr., this institution in East Jerusalem became home to most of the Dead Sea Scroll fragments and headquarters for the international team studying them. A long room, dubbed the scrollery, was set aside for the study and storage of the fragments. Now known as the Rockefeller Museum, the institution came under Israeli control after the Six-Day War in 1967. Access to the scrolls—and even to photographs of the scrolls—however, remained under the tight control of the international team, prompting *Biblical Archaeology Review* in 1989 to refer to the Rockefeller as "The Dead Sea Scrolls Prison."

FMC: In fact, the prices we paid for fragments were ridiculously low; and if we had paid ten times Kando's price for the large Psalms scroll from Cave 11, we still would have been the winners.

Two more tales of my role as a less than skilled negotiator in the pursuit of documents of the Jordan Rift. On May 11, 1962, Paul Lapp, the director of the American School of Oriental Research in Jerusalem and a former student of mine, wrote to me describing the discovery by Taʿâmireh of Aramaic papyri, probably dating to the fourth century B.C.E. Paul even suggested the date of c. 375 for one piece—about a quarter century early as it turned out. The papyrus was dated by a reference to Artaxerxes III (358-338 B.C.E.). Kando was asking 25,000 dinars ($70,000) for the papyri and bullae accompanying them.

Earlier the British Academy had put up some funds to buy Cave 4 scrolls. They were unexpended. De Vaux proposed to Kathleen Kenyon, director of the British School, that the money be used to purchase the papyri. Kenyon arranged for G. R. Driver of Oxford to come out to examine the material, and he recommended that not more than 5,000 pounds be spent for the fragmentary papyri. Kando laughed. De Vaux then asked Paul to write to me about possible American sources of

ELIZABETH HAY BECHTEL, a California philanthropist, funded the establishment of the Ancient Biblical Manuscript Center (ABMC), in Claremont, California. Her involvement with the Dead Sea Scrolls dated to 1960, when she provided the funds to purchase the Psalms Scroll from Qumrân Cave 11. She played an even greater role in the 1990s, albeit posthumously.

More than a decade earlier she had arranged for a set of photographs of the Dead Sea Scrolls, both published and unpublished, to be deposited in the ABMC. Before this could be done, however, Mrs. Bechtel had a falling out with the director, and she decided to keep a set for herself, which she deposited in the Huntington Library in San Marino, California. The ABMC had agreed in writing not to show the photos to anyone without permission of the scholar to whom that text had been assigned for publication, but Mrs. Bechtel was not a party to that agreement. In September 1991, four years after her death in 1987, William A. Moffett, the new library director, announced that all scholars could have access to the Huntington scroll photos, thus bringing a sudden end to the scholarly monopoly of the scrolls.

money for the papyri, suggesting that the lot should go for about 7,000 dinars, $20,000.

Acting again on behalf of the American Schools, I arrived in Jerusalem on November 14, 1962, with a check for $20,000 (7,000 dinars) in my pocket. On Saturday, November 17, I met with Kando and got my first glimpse of the material. There was one papyrus sealed with seven seals—obviously complete I wrongly thought. I found "Samaria" written on a fragment or two. What really struck my eye in the first minutes was a seal on a roll of papyrus stamped in paleo-Hebrew script. I could read *paḥat šōměrôn* (governor of Samaria) on the lower line of the seal immediately, and before the title three letters of a patronymic, *B-L-Ṭ*, *bet*, *lamed*, *ṭet*. I had no problem filling in the missing letters of the name; *balāṭu* was a well known Babylonian verbal element, familiar from the biblical name Sanballaṭ, properly Sinʾuballaṭ.⁹ The bulla belonged to the governor of Samaria, the son of Sanballaṭ. At this point, I could not suppress my excitement, and the price of the papyri went up £4,000.

On Sunday afternoon of the following day, at 3 p.m., Père de Vaux, Yusuf Saʿad and I were scheduled to sit down with Kando in the interior garden of the museum and negotiate the purchase of the papyri. When the time came, I was nowhere to be found, and Paul Lapp discovered me fast asleep in my room—exhausted from late hours, excitement and jet lag. I hastened over to the museum. Saʿad conducted the negotiations in English, Arabic and French. Kando feigned ignorance of any language but Arabic, but his mastery of English numbers was perfect.

As I did in the earlier negotiation for the Psalms Scroll, after long and heated haggling getting nowhere, I pulled out the check and threw it down on the table, saying this was all I had, take it or leave it. This time Kando did not take it. Finally I agreed to the price of £11,000, more than $30,000, £7,000 in cash and another £4,000 payable within a year. Where the additional money would come from I did not know, and I felt very uneasy until I got word from Mrs. Elizabeth Bechtel that she would foot the additional bill.

An unhappy postscript. Yusuf Saʿad not only knew the amount of the check I had in my pocket, he also knew that Mrs. Bechtel, who held him in great affection, would soon visit Jerusalem and probably would be good for the additional money. But I had no suspicions of

Yusuf, my helpful dragoman. Perhaps most distressing was my inability, owing to the exhaustion of my funds, to purchase the large hoards of coins found with the papyri and Samaritan bones. These were scattered, and although Dr. Yaʿaqov Meshorer has now published a large number of them, it is a pity they were split up and their provenience put into question.

We received the material on Monday, November 19. In the evening, the Lapps and I gathered in the scrollery of the museum to unroll the document with seven seals, the prize piece of the find. I gingerly cut the strings holding the seven seals in place. Humidifying the papyrus and using a fine brush with water, we coaxed the papyrus open and began unrolling it turn by turn. Six turns were unwound and no writing appeared. It seemed I had paid a fortune for a blank piece of papyrus. On the seventh turn, however, a bold line of script appeared. When the top line was reached, we read a date formula, "On the 20th of Adar, year 2, the accession year of Darius the king, in Samaria..." We were very lucky. It was a double date formula, by Arses, who died in the second year of his reign, and by the accession year of Darius III.

After going to the library to check the calendars of the Achaemenid kings, we could assign a precise date to the papyrus—March 19, 335 B.C.E. We were also very unlucky. Less than half of the papyrus, a slave conveyance, was preserved. A number of years would pass before we could reconstruct the legal formulae of a slave conveyance sufficiently well to fill in lacunae and discover the full

PAUL LAPP. The director of the American School of Oriental Research in Jerusalem in the early 1960s, Lapp informed Cross in May 1962 of the discovery of Aramaic papyri and bullae (clay seal impressions) in the Wâdī ed-Dâliyeh, about 10 miles north of Jericho. Lapp helped arrange a meeting between Cross and Kando for the purchase of the finds. The negotiators eventually agreed on a price of £11,000 (more than $30,000)—more than the $20,000 Cross was prepared to pay on the spot, but considerably less than the $70,000 Kando had initially demanded.

contents of this papyrus, published as Samaria Papyrus 1. The papyri are all badly preserved, having been a feast for hungry worms after the bones of the massacred patricians from Samaria were dry and clean.

A second tale. Early in 1967, a Washington law firm wrote to me, and later its representatives made a visit to Cambridge to discuss Qumrân scrolls for sale. The firm was wealthy and respectable, as Washington law firms go, so I took their claim seriously that they were middlemen for persons in Jordan and Beirut who had complete Qumrân scrolls for sale. The scrolls were purportedly from Cave 11. Rumors about Cave 11 material that had never come into scholarly hands had been circulating for a decade—and indeed circulate to this day.

Acting for the American Schools scroll committee, I set out again for Jerusalem on March 3 with two tasks to accomplish, the public task of attempting to found a new American School of Oriental Research in Beirut and the private task of negotiating for the purchase of the scroll or scrolls being offered in Beirut. I made clear to the authorities in Jerusalem that whatever scrolls the American Schools acquired would be returned to Jerusalem and the Rockefeller.

From March 5 to 11, 1967, I traveled about Lebanon looking for an excavation site for the projected new school, deciding that Paleo-Tyre, mainland Tyre, was ideal. I was met in Beirut by a representative of the Washington law firm, by the director of a major American public museum, and by a certain rogue named Wendell Phillips. They stayed at the Phoenicia; I stayed in a small waterfront hotel whose name I have forgotten. I had been given a phone number in Beirut before I left home, and now came the day to call it. Someone answered in good English and asked for my number. Later he called and asked if I could identify myself. I said that I had his phone number and was known to the representative of the Washington firm. What more was necessary? Whom did I know in Beirut? I mentioned Maurice Chehab, the director of antiquities (which didn't get a laugh), Bill Holladay then at the Protestant Divinity School, Henri Seyrig at the French Institute, Dimitri Baramki at the American University, Professor Rustum, and so on. He hung up.

Later in the day the same person, who remained nameless, called and said they were satisfied I was who I claimed to be and proposed that I meet them that night at 11 p.m. under an arch in the Old Suq of Beirut—alone. I argued that my associates should come along. To no avail. So I found my way by cab to the designated rendezvous, where the cab driver left me after asking if I really wished to be left alone in such a place. After he left, I debated with myself. Should I stand in a shadow or in plain view on the street? It occurred to me that the person or persons whom I was to meet might figure that I had come prepared to pay the $1 million or more asked per scroll and that they might take unpleasant measures to extract money from me. The place was perfect for a robbery. So I thought. No one was to be seen. It was very dark. Garbage littered the walkways under the arches. One body more or less might not be noticed for days.

After a very long time passed—perhaps ten minutes—a Mercedes came into sight, rolled past me standing in the archway, and circled out of sight again. A few minutes later it came back into view and paused in front of me. A door was opened, and I was invited into the back seat by a silver-haired gentleman who spoke French-accented English. I immediately noticed a man with his head hidden under the dash sitting to the right of the driver. His brachycephalic skull was familiar. So I said, "Greetings, O Kando, how are you?" (*Marḥaba ya-Kando, kêf el-ḥâl?*). He rose, grinning, thanked God several times, asked me about my health, and shortly ran out of Arabic I understood.

We were taken to a grand mansion where the banker—the driver of the car—lived. Kando showed me several boxes of fragments, some from Cave 11, others of the Bar Kokhba era, including a Greek contract or two. But, he explained, he had a great scroll to sell worth millions of dollars.

HS: He had the Temple Scroll?

FMC: Yes, but he did not have it with him. But to resume my conversation with Kando. Why did he not have the great scroll with him? I asked. Further, the Washington contact had sworn to me that he had several great scrolls. Well, he had at least one. And the fragments, the remarkable fragments he had brought. I said I was not interested in his expletive-deleted fragments. He then proposed that I come to Jerusalem with him. He would sell me the scroll. I said that my donor was a busy man who had come to Beirut. Why had he not brought the scroll or scrolls as promised? I had missed classes at the university; I had spent the donor's good money to come to Beirut.

Show the scroll to me here in Beirut. Go get it if necessary. But he insisted that he was afraid to bring it out and that big men (I gathered the Taʿâmireh elders) wouldn't let him take it to Beirut. After a long evening, I realized that he did not have the scroll with him. I told him that my former student, Paul Lapp, the professor at the American School, would negotiate for me. He knew Paul, who had been present at the negotiations for the Dâliyeh papyri. Show the scroll to him, and he would authenticate it and get in touch with me. Perhaps I would return to Jerusalem in the summer and buy his scroll.

In June 1967, the Six-Day War broke out. The Old City was united with greater Jerusalem, and Bethlehem came under the jurisdiction of Israel. On June 8, less than a month after my visit with Kando, Yigael Yadin, who had been negotiating with Kando by way of another American middleman, a Virginia clergyman, sent an army colonel to Kando's home. He asked Kando for the scroll, and Kando, the cobbler, handed over a shoe box. The officer brought it to Yadin, and inside Yadin found the Temple Scroll. Kando received $105,000 for the document, far less than he had hoped but more than he deserved.[10] He had violated the agreement that had given him immunity over the years and sought millions abroad. In the end, everything turned out well. The Temple Scroll provided a suitable climax to Yadin's career, an appropriate anticlimax in Kando's list of financial triumphs and a brief adventure for me.

HS: The Virginia clergyman's name was Joe Uhrig.

FMC: Is that his name? I never knew it.

HS: Yadin called him Mr. Z to protect his identity. Actually Mr. Z was Joe Uhrig, an early televangelist.

FMC: I talked with Yadin shortly after he acquired the Temple Scroll. I described to him in detail the materials I had seen in Kando's possession in Beirut. I also expressed my concern that having Kando arrested and his scroll seized might end the flow of materials into scholarly hands and lead to the scattering of scrolls or scroll fragments in the foreign antiquities markets. Yadin answered, I cannot tell you the whole story, but you may be certain that my actions will

ENTRANCE TO MUGHÂRET ʾABŪ-SHINJEH, the cave at Wâdī ed-Dâliyeh where the Samaria papyri were found. In the picture (above opposite), seven seal impressions cling to a papyrus from Wâdī ed-Dâliyeh, the prize piece of the collection. When Cross brought it to the scrollery of the Rockefeller Museum for study, he first cut the strings that held the seals in place and succeeded in opening the papyrus by humidifying it and brushing it with a fine coat of water. When he had unrolled six turns without discovering any writing, he began to fear he had paid a small fortune for a blank papyrus.

With the seventh turn, however, script appeared. The top line contained a date corresponding to March 19, 335 B.C.E., the second year of the reign of the Persian king Darius III. The document, less than half of which was preserved, proved to be a slave conveyance.

A second important seal impression from Wâdī ed-Dâliyeh (below opposite) reads, "[Belonging to Yašaʿ]yahû, son of [San]ballaṭ governor of Samaria." Attached to it is the remnant of a contract regarding the sale of a vineyard, probably dating to the reign of Artaxerxes III (358-338 B.C.E.).

not alter any arrangement with Kando. The materials will continue to flow in. This is my rough memory of Yadin's reply. I gathered from Yadin's assurances that Kando, ever the wily conspirator, had been party to the seizure and his own arrest.

HS: Was he actually arrested?

FMC: I think so. At least this was the report I received. But if so, he was soon released. He was not convicted of illegal possession of the scroll.

HS: Was he ever formally charged?

FMC: I don't know. My memory is that he was put in jail briefly, sufficiently long for Nelson Glueck to become outraged at Kando's treatment, secure him a lawyer and demand that he be remunerated fairly for the scroll. I think Nelson's sense of justice in this instance was misplaced. Kando, if my knowledge of the man serves me well, figured that if he sold the scroll to the Israelis, it would put him in bad odor, indeed in physical danger, at home. Obviously, he was interested in selling the scroll to any buyer who would pay his price. He had been negotiating on both sides of the Green Line, so to speak—with my group in Beirut and Washington, with Yadin's group in Israel

YIGAEL YADIN wore many hats besides the excavator's *chapeau* he donned for this photo. As the foremost Israeli archaeologist, he is best known for his excavations at Masada and Hazor. He was also chief of staff of the Israeli army during the 1948 War of Independence and a politician (late in life he served as deputy prime minister under Menachem Begin). Following in the footsteps of his father, Eliezer L. Sukenik, Yadin obtained four of the scrolls from Cave 1 at Qumrân. He later negotiated, without success, for the purchase of the longest of all the scrolls, the Temple Scroll, which was discovered in 1956 in Cave 11. When the Israelis captured Bethlehem in 1967, Yadin sent an army officer to Kando's home. Kando removed a shoe box from beneath his floor containing the scroll. Although he had held the scroll illegally, Kando was paid $105,000—"far less than he had hoped but more than he deserved," says Cross.

and Virginia. When Bethlehem came under Israeli jurisdiction, Kando made the best deal he could, including in it certain *sub rosa* safeguards.

HS: And arranged his own arrest?

FMC: This appears to me to be the simplest explanation of the contradictory accounts of these events and especially of the assurances Yadin gave me. A historian always prefers parsimonious explanations, even if they must be set aside for more complicated ones when new facts come to light.

HS: It has been about 25 years since then, and no more scrolls have surfaced.

FMC: Well, rumors of scrolls, or at least of a fragmentary document, continue to circulate, and have recently become persistent. I know nothing firsthand; but I'll not be surprised if new material turns up.

HS: Do you remember when you first met J. T. Milik?

FMC: Yes, vividly. He returned to Jerusalem and the scrollery in the early fall of 1953. When we were first introduced, he tried several of his languages on me without much success. In delightful, sometimes hilarious English he explained that he had had little occasion to speak English but had learned a great deal of English from reading "zee crime fictions," mostly of the hard-boiled type, I gathered. The scrollery became English and French speaking. Milik's English quickly improved but never completely lost its Polish flavor. He wore a cassock in those days, with a dribble of tobacco ash down the front.

Milik was, and is, an intensely shy person. But thanks to our long hours at work together, we soon became good friends. In the first year, we wrote two papers together and began a joint project of exploration in the Judean Buqêʿah. He was dour, even melancholy, in demeanor. But he had a quick, infectious sense of humor, and when he suddenly saw the humor in a situation or comment, he would break out giggling—I don't know what other word to use—to the delight of his companions. Milik does not communicate easily with outsiders or people he does not know well. He sometimes writes letters but rarely responds to letters. Before his death Starcky acted as a go-between for Milik and people who tried to communicate with him.

HS: What was it like working together, you seven or eight people?

FMC: We worked easily and well together for the most part. We shared the excitement of each other's discoveries. We went on an occasional holiday together, especially Milik, Starcky and I, and later Strugnell. The only trouble in the scrollery came with John Allegro. He was jovial enough, but we soon learned that he could not be trusted. I have often described him as amoral—one of the few amoral people I have known. Whatever he wanted to be true was true. He was also a limited and sloppy scholar, and in a context where everyone worked cooperatively on all the manuscripts (in the early days) or helped each other, adding to each other's manuscripts (after lots were assigned), he made a poor colleague.

The volume of Cave 4 texts he edited[11] is the worst in the series. It would have been even worse if others in the scrollery had not caught a number of wrong joins he had made and corrected them before publication. John Strugnell's 113-page review of the volume is actually the *editio princeps*.[12] It is painful reading. The one good thing to be said is that Allegro published quickly. But that is only if one wishes to have a bad edition quickly rather than a good and reliable edition slowly. Soon there was more trouble. He published a pirate edition

FATHER JOZEF MILIK, a Polish cleric dubbed by *Time* magazine "the fastest man with a fragment," received the lion's share of the Cave 4 materials for publication. Conservators today cringe when they see pictures of Milik handling 2,000-year-old fragments with his bare hands while smoking a cigarette. Cross praises Milik's skills, calling him the most gifted member of the original editorial team. Even Milik, however, was not up to the sheer size of the task, and after much prodding, he gave the remainder of his fragments to other scholars for publication. Having left the priesthood and married, Milik now lives in Paris.

of the Copper Scroll, which had been assigned to Milik. He sold pho-tographs from the scrollery archives to a commercial agency in England. And then there were the stories he gave to the tabloids, para-noid ravings about Vatican control of the scrolls. He knew very well that what he fed the press was untrue.

HS: What was his motivation?

FMC: He told me. Money. He did not bother with excuses. When he returned to the scrollery after a good deal of this slander had been printed, I confronted him. I said, John, were you correctly quoted in these interviews and newspaper stories? He admitted that he had been quoted more or less accurately. I then expressed my scorn. I said I knew that he knew that much of the Cave 4 material had come into my hands first—the excavated material of Cave 4, several batches I had purchased and examined before they were seen by anyone else. Indeed, a good part of the two large lots opened and prepared in the fall of 1953 went through my hands first; Milik and I divided the labors.

FATHERS JEAN STARCKY (rear) **AND MILIK** study fragments in the scrollery under the watchful eye of Frank Cross. Cross has fond memories of almost all of his colleagues. This photo, like the one opposite, shows how carelessly the scrolls were handled in the early days, when fragments were joined together with cel-lophane tape, which eats away at the material, or pressed between plates of glass, trapping moisture and further damaging the documents.

I asked him angrily, how can you claim that all this stuff is controlled by the Vatican and is seen first only by Catholic priests? He grinned at me and said, "It pays." Paranoia sells. I had no further dealings with Allegro after this encounter. He was a friendly and engaging person, but he was bent.

HS: Was it fun being together?

FMC: Oh, yes. As I mentioned we sometimes took holidays together or went on journeys to visit ancient sites. In the spring of 1954, we went on excavation at Qumrân, taking a vacation from our tedious, indoor labors. I remember one lovely day, drinking Italian wine—*Lacrima Cristi*—in a garden in Jericho with Starcky and Milik. They were good companions. I remember many nights when Skehan and I and another companion or two would go late over to the Aẓ-Ẓahra Hotel behind the American School of Oriental Research. There was a lovely garden over there filled with pepper trees. We would each have a bottle of Dutch beer and talk into the night.

HS: How long were you there?

FMC: I spent three full sabbatical years there. In addition, in the early years I came to Jerusalem every summer for three or four months.

JOHN STRUGNELL, shown here outside the Rockefeller Museum in the 1950s, came to Jerusalem in 1954 fresh from Oxford. He had no idea at the time that he would spend the rest of his career working on the Dead Sea Scrolls. Strugnell later joined the faculty at Harvard Divinity School and became editor-in-chief of the scrolls publication team in 1987.

To his credit, Strugnell expanded the team to include Jewish scholars and women, and he convinced Milik to reassign many of his manuscripts. He was undone by an interview he granted an Israeli journalist in 1991, in which he urged Jews to convert to Christianity and called Judaism "a horrible religion." The subsequent public uproar forced his removal as chief editor. Strugnell remains on the team, however, and continues to control a block of Cave 4 documents.

Later I came sporadically for longer or shorter stays as required by my work. It was not easy for those of us with professorships and young children to spend the long stints of time in Jerusalem demanded by the work. For this reason Skehan and I took biblical texts, which were easier to identify and edit. Those who could reside permanently in Jerusalem with research appointments—Milik, Starcky and Strugnell (in the first years)—took lots consisting of sectarian, apocryphal or unknown documents.

HS: Would you have liked to work on some of the sectarian material?

FMC: Sure. In fact in the early years we all worked on everything. And I have published a paper or two on sectarian documents. I would have loved to edit unknown and sectarian documents. So much of the material is new and surprising. And, if the truth were known, I had never been interested in textual criticism until I landed in the scrollery. The unknown documents, sectarian or otherwise, pose problems that few appreciate. A scholar can identify a scribal hand and some manuscript traits, such as color of leather, distance between dry-line rulings of the leather and so on, and on the basis of these characters, assemble a group of fragments belonging to a discrete manuscript. Perhaps he can make a few material joins. Usually, though, worms have conspired to obliterate the edges.

From the content of these scattered fragments, one must determine the subject matter of the document, the structure or plot, and reconstruct the sequence of columns, usually with few fragments preserving an overlap of more than one badly preserved column. Sometimes damage forms patterns—like paper doll cutouts—and this gives a clue to the sequence of the fragments. All in all, the task is incredibly challenging and requires the imagination of a genius and the patience of a drudge to complete. I have always had sympathy for someone like Milik who received the bulk of the difficult texts. He was, and is, the most gifted member of the team.

HS: Most gifted in what way?

FMC: He was the most gifted at putting together and making sense of unknown documents. Many documents are, in effect, Milik's creations. If he had a fault, it was excess of imagination. He was an instinctive paleographer with a good eye for form. He wasn't a systematic or scientific paleographer, but he did not need to be. He could spot a scribe's hand on a fragment that belonged to this or that group of fragments (incipient manuscripts so to speak) faster than most of us. And he had the hands of hundreds of scribes in his head.

HS: Do you have any recollection of how the assignments were made?

FMC: Yes, the team together with de Vaux arrived at a consensus. Basically, we each chose what we wanted to edit, or to put a better face on it, what we thought we were best fitted to edit. There was some horse trading. Usually the scholars who came first had first choice. I had first choice of the biblical materials; but I saw to it that Skehan received some exciting material, namely the paleo-Hebrew manuscripts. Milik was given the most interesting nonbiblical materials. Starcky, an Aramaist, took most of the Aramaic documents—but not the Enoch material, which went to Milik. Strugnell inherited a great number of documents handed over to him by Milik and others as well as hymnic and wisdom literature, which he wanted. I gave him some biblical paraphrases. Most of us got a good part of what we wanted or were best fitted to edit. It was a rational and friendly process.

HS: What about Allegro?

FMC: John Allegro wanted the *pešer* manuscripts (biblical commentaries), which, together with a small miscellany of other pieces, were given to him. His was the smallest lot. When he began his attacks on the team and made his allegations of a Vatican plot, his relations with the team deteriorated. But there was never a question of taking the manuscripts away from him. That would have violated scholarly ethics. He had prepared his material, and he had a right to publish it.

HS: What were his accusations against the Vatican?

FMC: He claimed that the Vatican, through priests on the international team, had first access to the materials and suppressed, or was in a position to suppress, any material that might threaten the Christian faith. Edmund Wilson's popular book, which first made the Dead Sea Scrolls famous, had suggested that Jewish lore in the scrolls that anticipated Christian teaching tended to undermine Christian notions of the uniqueness of some Christian institutions or teachings. His knowledge of Christianity was colored by the Presbyterian orthodoxy of his Princeton background. The apologetic tradition of such orthodoxy ignored or denied continuities between Judaism and the Jewish "heresy" that came to be called Christianity. But Allegro's conspiracy claims were of a different order. He hinted at dark secrets in the scrolls, which, if aired, would shatter Christian or Jewish beliefs.

HS: Well, even today people frequently ask if there is something in the scrolls that is going to undermine the faith of either Christians or Jews. More often it is asked about Christians. Is there anything to that?

FMC: No, there is nothing to it. The scrolls are documents composed by Jews with a fervent, near fanatical faith. Their literature can't

JOHN M. ALLEGRO of the University of Manchester, the maverick of the group, joined the team in 1953 and quickly made himself the odd man out. In a broadcast on the BBC, Allegro recklessly linked Jesus to the Qumrân sect. He also accused the Vatican of controlling the interpretation of the scrolls through the Catholic scholars on the editorial team. When Cross, a Protestant who had been the first to see many of the Cave 4 fragments, challenged him, Allegro cheerfully admitted he had concocted his charges to make money. Thereafter, Cross had no further dealings with him.

Allegro went on to publish a pirate version of a unique text called the Copper Scroll (which had been assigned to Milik) and led an excavation in the Judean desert in search of treasures he believed were listed in the Copper Scroll. Allegro's volume on Cave 4 fragments, Cross says, is "the weakest in the series."

threaten Christianity (or Judaism) any more than the books of the Old Testament or, to be more precise, any more than apocalyptic works of the Hebrew Bible like the Book of Daniel can.

HS: Well, we have talked about the Son of God text. Here is a reference to the son of God. It is there at Qumrân a hundred years before Jesus came on the scene. To the person on the street it would appear to indicate that the whole idea of the son of God was in the air, pre-Christian, and that it was something Christians picked up from that milieu—and that, in fact, Jesus may not be the Son of God. That's what's going through the mind of the person in the street.

FMC: Perhaps I should amend my reply to say that there is nothing in the scrolls that will harm the faith of an informed Christian or Jew. A casual reading of the New Testament will make clear that the claim of New Testament writers is that Jesus is the Messiah prophesied in Scriptures (i.e., the Hebrew Bible), and they identify him with the titles of the Davidic kings and the future Davidid, the messiah *par excellence*—and indeed with the epithets of the Priestly Messiah. The sobriquet "Son of God" is one borne by the Davidic kings.[13] Scholars have long debated whether this "high Christology" of the Judean royal house is meant to claim divine kingship or points to an "adoptionist" royal ideology. Incidentally, both understandings of the title "son of God" may be found in the New Testament.

In my view, there are two basic theologies or ideologies of kingship in Israel. One is that the king is the son of God. The other is that the king has an eternal covenant with the deity. Both amount to the same thing in Israel. Both adoption and covenant are legal substitutes for kinship. They place the obligations and benefits of kinship on both the deity and the king. In adoption procedures, you declare someone "my son," "today I have begotten you," and he becomes, by a legal fiction, blood kin. So the Lord addresses the son of David, "Thou art my son. Today I have begotten you" (Psalm 2:7). Alternately, one can speak of the Davidic covenant with the Lord that imposes the duties of kinship on both parties. In short, the language of divine sonship or kinship is already in the Hebrew Bible, and it comes as no surprise to find terms like "son of God" and "son of the Most High" in the pseudo-Daniel fragment from Qumrân.

THE SON OF GOD TEXT. This Aramaic fragment, given the siglum 4Q246, refers to a future deliverer, who "will be called son of God" and "will be called son of the Most High." Both titles and the verb parallel Luke's Infancy Narrative, in which the angel Gabriel announces to Mary that she will bear the Christ child (Luke 1:26-38). The term "son of God" occurs several times in the Hebrew Bible, usually to describe a ruler as an adopted child of God, but this fragment is the first to use the term in reference to a future redeemer and shows that the Gospel writers drew on the language and imagery of Jewish messianic literature.

As a matter of fact, in 14th-century Ugarit, the Canaanite epics use as a standard epithet of their king, "son of ʾEl" (*bn ʾIl*), eerily close to the Aramaic *barēh dî ʾEl*, "son of God." There is some evidence that in Canaanite royal ideology the king was fully divinized (as in Egypt and in Mesopotamia in some periods). In Israel, I do not believe there was true divination of the king even in eras of syncretism. Israel's kingship was limited by the prophets, who were perennial critics of the royal house, and by the rejection of the notion that kingship belonged to the orders of creation. In Israel, the ideal age was pre-monarchic. Israel's epic sources reach a climax in the age of Moses. And the Deuteronomic and Priestly sources of the Pentateuch nostalgically attempt to reconstruct the institutions and legal lore of premonarchic Israel.

Another example you might have chosen with the potential to shake up Christians is the communion meal at Qumrân, a ritual enactment of the Messianic Banquet of the New Covenant. Here, the priestly messiah presides and serves; the Davidic or lay messiah is in attendance. Again, the notion of a Messianic Banquet of the New Age is familiar from prophetic literature and later Jewish literature.[14] The Pharisees had communion meals, which were similar. So again we must recognize a Jewish-Christian continuum.

The New Testament communion meal is eschatological, anticipating the Messianic Banquet, the feast of the New Covenant. It may be described as eating the bread and the wine of (the new) David as found in the Didache. Paul's language of eating the body and drinking the blood of the Messiah who is sacrificed is strange and novel and its meaning debated. Some see it as a poetic identification of Jesus with the paschal lamb. Jesus is called "the Lamb." Others see it as sublimated theophagy. And so on. At Ugarit, we actually have a text describing a mythic scene in which a young woman comes upon her lover, the young god, who lies dead, and "she eats his flesh without a knife, drinks his blood without a cup."[15]

HS: But we don't have that in the Hebrew Bible.

FMC: No, never in the Hebrew Bible—nor in the Apocrypha nor in the Pseudepigrapha nor in the Qumrân scrolls.

HS: We do have it in the New Testament?

FMC: "This is my body; this is my blood."

HS: Where do you think that comes from?

FMC: I suspect it is a transformation of a lost mythic theme. But to return to our discussion; an informed Christian or an informed Jew does not argue that New Testament Christianity is *sui generis*, radically unique. Christianity emerges from Judaism in full historic continuity with the thought, faith, institutions and hopes of Judaism. The Bible of the earliest Christians was the Hebrew Bible. They did not have a New Testament; and even when the writings that form the New

Testament were being written they were not yet authoritative.

HS: But for many Christians, there's a problem at the intersection of history and faith.

FMC: Yes. I think the same is true of Jews. It is a problem for religions whose revelation or sacred scripture is historical.

HS: The New Testament takes the sonship (of God) a little further along. It is no longer an adopted sonship but rather a genealogical sonship from birth—Canaanite royal mythology popping up again?

FMC: There may also be some influence from the ontological thinking in the Greek world. Sons (and daughters) of gods were very much at home in the Greek world. In the early church, reflected already in the New Testament, an ontological understanding of the expression "son of God" evidently replaced the vocational or legal understanding of the epithet, which is primary in the Bible.

HS: You posit a shift in the New Testament from the halakhic to the ontological.

FMC: Yes, in the later strata of the New Testament. I should not have thought to use the term halakhic, but you are quite right. Later, in the Catholic Church, you have the development of the trinitarian formula, the three masks or "persons" of God. For the Christian in the street, or better, for the Christian in the back pew of the church, the traditional epithet "son of God" is read through the lens of the Old Catholic confessions.

HS: You spoke of informed Christians, and I would guess that in your terms that means no more than 2 percent of the faithful. But looking at it simplistically, from the point of view of the person in the pew, Jesus either was or was not the Son of God. If I understand you correctly, you are suggesting a more spiritual than literal understanding of that concept.

FMC: I should like to be more precise in our language. I am not suggesting a spiritual understanding, if this expression means what it usually does, namely an allegorical interpretation. The simple believer who says that Jesus was or was not the Son of God is actually thinking in sophisticated ontological (or physical) terms, Greek categories. The church, orthodox or fundamentalist, often encourages this anachronistic approach to scriptural texts. My concern is to pursue the historical exegesis of expressions like the "son of God." What did the expression mean in the several stages of development, in its transformations?

I think the late New Testament understanding—the ontological— is not part of Jesus' thinking or of Paul's belief or the thinking of his early followers. For the person who supposes that the Holy Spirit is the physical father of Jesus, I think it would be disturbing to discover that Paul is unaware of the doctrine of the virgin birth; or to read the genealogies of Jesus carefully and discover that they all trace his Davidic lineage through Joseph. What is the meaning of a genealogy that goes through Joseph if in fact Jesus is not the son of Joseph? The testimony of the New Testament, if examined historically and critically, is complex, with different strata and a mixture of understandings of messianic titles.

HS: Are you saying that any Christian who takes history seriously has to interpret the New Testament in a symbolic way rather than a literal way?

FMC. I should say rather that when an author uses symbols, we should recognize them as symbols, and when he speaks literally, we should recognize that he means to be taken literally. Again, let me stress that I wish interpretation of biblical literature to be historical and critical, an attempt to understand what the ancient author meant to say. If the author of Revelation calls Jesus the bright morning star, how are we to understand this expression? In this case it is clearly poetic language, traditional language used to describe the priestly messiah. Jesus is not a star, not even a superstar. The author of the Gospel of Matthew took the star image literally (or the tradition he drew upon took it literally), and the moving star of Bethlehem, which is an embarrassment to moderns, was invented.

The scrolls underline the continuities between Christianity and Judaism. Often these continuities require that Christians reinterpret the New Testament or Christian tradition in Jewish or Old Testament categories, not in the Greek categories of medieval Christianity. This prospect is not always welcome. Many conservative Jews are also uneasy about these continuities. In light of their experience with Christianity, they would like to push Christianity as far away from Judaism as possible.

HS: Is this Jewish uneasiness related to the continuities, or is it related to the possibility that the sanctity of the Masoretic text will be undermined?

FMC: It is true that some are concerned about the possibility of a variety of textual traditions alongside the Masoretic text to which they are accustomed and which they had assumed goes back unchanged to the biblical authors. The problem is not serious. I am reminded of a young biblical scholar of rigid Calvinistic stock who discovered that there were variations in manuscripts of both the Old and the New Testament. How then could he feel secure in what was, in fact, the inspired and infallible word of God? He decided that the text used in Calvin's commentaries was authoritative and maintained without error by the Holy Spirit. The ultraorthodox Jew can proceed the same way and fix on the biblical text of Maimonides as authoritative. Both positions reject historical approaches to the text of the Bible.

HS: But isn't there a difference between problems faced by informed Jews and problems faced by informed Christians? In the case of Christianity, we are talking about a threat to central doctrine. If you have variations between, let's say, the Old Greek text and the Masoretic text, these are mostly nonideological. But the difference between interpreting the expression "son of God" to mean that Jesus was the actual, physical son of God and the adopted son of God, a legal fiction, is different—especially in light of its history for 1,500 years and more.

FMC: The threat to the orthodox doctrine of the divinity of Jesus comes not from the appearance of the epithet "son of God" at Qumrân. As I have noted, this was a title of the Judean kings. Jews who followed Jesus claimed that the Old Testament title of the Davidic king and the Jewish epithets of the messiah were to be applied to Jesus. He fulfilled the old promises. He was the Messiah.

The threat comes from historical exegesis, which traces the slow transformation of the expression from an adoptionist interpretation to an ontological (or physical) interpretation. And even this does not threaten orthodoxy in churches that place equal authority in church tradition and in Scripture. In effect they can say that the tradition affirming the ontological meaning has ultimate authority over the meaning derived from the historical exegesis of Scripture alone. Protestants, with their insistence on *sola scriptura* and their rejection of nonliteral or spiritualizing exegesis, have a more difficult time. But even Protestants can say that the final meaning of the title in certain New Testament texts is authoritative—interpretation by the latest developments in the canon or, with a bow to tradition, by the understanding of those who fixed the canon. This is so-called canonical exegesis, in my opinion a dangerously ahistorical approach to the Bible and, in the hands of some conservative scholars, a dangerous, if somewhat respectable, mutation of fundamentalist approaches to Scripture.

It is possible to argue that for informed Jews some problems created by the Qumrân texts are as serious, if not more serious, than for informed Christians. Halakhic decisions of the rabbis are based on the Masoretic text, not to mention cabalistic and Midrashic elaborations and exegeses. If one reading, the Masoretic reading, is the basis for a halakhic decision, and a Qumrân or Greek text provides a variant reading that, after critical analysis, proves to be superior, this would be a very serious matter. Indeed, the Halakhic Epistle (MMT) at Qumrân is at the center of a debate about halakhic issues, some of which presume a biblical text at variance with the Masoretic text. One of the chief reasons for the promulgation of the Rabbinic Recension was to produce an immutable foundation for halakhic decisions.

HS: But it is not important to many Jews today whether pouring liquid from a pure vessel into an impure vessel makes the liquid in the pure vessel impure because the impurity from the impure vessel jumps up with the stream of liquid as it pours.

FMC: I think you are mistaken. Not only do I think such matters are of serious concern to the ultraorthodox, I think even a learned orthodox Jew like the late Rabbi Soloveitchik would argue that strict attention to the laws of purity and halakhic decisions about minutiae are important. Such problems would be dismissed not because they are unimportant but because of the tradition that the Masoretic text is authoritative, and the question of the original text of books of the Hebrew Bible is not to be pursued. This is the Jewish equivalent of the Catholic doctrine that gives tradition an authoritative voice in the handling of Scripture.

HS: You mentioned that Jews might also be troubled because of the continuities that the Qumrân community demonstrates between Judaism and Christianity.

FMC: I was thinking of two aspects of the matter. First, the history of the religious persecution of Jews by Christians has been such that anything that pushes Judaism closer to Christianity is to be resisted. This is less a scholarly issue than an emotional one. But a very powerful one. The second aspect has to do with the scholarly task of reconstructing the history of Judaism in the last centuries of the Second Temple and placing Christian origins in this continuum.

Rabbinic, specifically tannaitic, Judaism, is presented in traditional sources as monolithic, going back relatively unchanged, if not to Sinai, at least to the Second Temple period. Rival parties to the Pharisaic party are mentioned, but, with the possible exception of the Sadducees, they appear marginal and of no historical or religious importance. This traditional picture of late pre-Christian Judaism was hardly modified in the long scholarly tradition of which George Foot Moore, cited above, is an example. Moore emphatically excluded the apocalyptic movement and its works from the mainstream of "normative" Judaism.

These ideas had begun to change even before the appearance of the Qumrân literature. Now this process must be accelerated, and a new historical picture of Judaism in the last centuries of the Second Temple must come into focus. There was, no doubt, a strain in the Judaism of this period that anticipated the Judaism of the Mishnah; but other forms of Judaism were also very much alive and probably dominant. The apocalyptic movement was particularly powerful and for a period of time was taken up by elements of the Sadducees (the Essenes) and by many of the Pharisees, who included Daniel in their canon.

HS: But isn't it true that apocalyptic Judaism did not survive the Roman destruction of the Temple?

FMC: Obviously it survives in the Jewish-Christian community. But if you argue that it wholly disappeared in the Pharisaic Jewish communities that survived the First Jewish Revolt against Rome, you have some formidable scholarly foes. Gershon Scholem argues just the reverse.

HS: There is a strain of Jewish mysticism—

FMC: Let me find a quote from Scholem:

> I must preface a word intended to correct a widespread mis-conception. I am referring to the distortion of historical cir-cumstances, equally popular among Jewish and Christian schol-ars, which lies in denying the continuation of the apocalyptic tradition in rabbinic Judaism. This distortion of intellectual his-tory is quite understandable in terms of the anti-Jewish inter-ests of Christian scholars as well as the anti-Christian interests of Jewish ones. It was in keeping with the tendencies of the for-mer group to regard Judaism only as the antechamber of Christianity and to see it as moribund once it had brought forth Christianity...Their view led to the conception of a genuine con-tinuation of Messianism via the Apocalyptists in the new world of Christianity. But the other group too paid tribute to their own prejudices. They were the great Jewish scholars of the nine-teenth and early twentieth centuries who to a great extent deter-mined the popular image of Judaism. In view of their concept of a purified and rational Judaism, they could only applaud the attempt to eliminate or liquidate Apocalypticism from the realm of Judaism. Without regrets they left the claim of apocalyptic continuity to a Christianity which, to their minds, gained noth-ing on that account. Historical truth was the price paid for the prejudices of both camps.[16]

HS: You said that the Qumrân material is not a threat to informed Christians. Does it undermine the faith of uninformed Christians and their overly simple understanding of Gospel texts?

FMC: I think it will trouble the person who has been led by the clergy or by Christian polemics to believe that Judaism is moribund and Christianity wholly new, or to suppose that Jesus invented the idea of the communion meal, that he first thought up the notion of the Twelve, that the New Covenant is novel and not a renewed covenant (as the Hebrew means), that the titles Jesus held as the Christ or Messiah were unanticipated in Jewish messianic Apocalypticism (or earlier in the Hebrew Bible). In short, I think anyone who has accepted claims of the discontinuity between Christianity and Judaism uncritically, or who has been brainwashed by the perennial tendency of the Christian pulpit to compare Judaism unfavorably with Christianity, may be shocked and may have to rethink his faith if he pays serious attention to the literature of Qumrân and of Hellenistic Judaism. But these problems will soon evaporate if he pays equal attention to the historical-critical study of the New Testament. What is difficult really is learning to think historically about Scripture and church tradition.

HS: There is another theological concept we haven't mentioned but which is much debated. That's resurrection. For a time we were told that at Qumrân there was no belief in the resurrection of the dead. Now we know that is not true.

FMC: Hippolytus (*Refutatio* 9, 27) told us that the Essenes believed in the resurrection of the dead. Arguments from silence are very dangerous. We also have been told by students of apocalypticism that the Daniel literature has no doctrine of the Messiah. The Son of God text, which is part of the Daniel literature, puts the lie to that argument.

HS: How does the Qumrân material affect faith in the Resurrection of Jesus?

FMC: I see no reason for it to affect faith in the Christian doctrine one way or another. In the Hebrew Bible, the only open, explicit mention of resurrection is in Daniel 12:1-3. Passages in Ezekiel and Isaiah are often interpreted as testimony to a doctrine of resurrection.[17] I personally do not think they are. I think they are talking about the resurrection or revival of the community of Israel. The great hymn to the suffering servant in Isaiah 52:13-53:12 is in this category, I believe, prophesying the resurrection of Israel that it may fulfill its vocation as servant of the Lord. It is not resurrection in the apocalyptic sense of resurrection of the body of the individual. We know that the doctrine was at home among the Pharisees and the Essenes. However, there is no reference in the Qumrân literature to the Resurrection of the Messiah—only to the birth or coming of the Messiah.

HS: Let me be more specific. There are at least two kinds of resurrection: (1) the Resurrection of Jesus, which was or was not a historical event; and (2) the anticipated resurrection at the end of days.

FMC: The New Testament authors believed that they lived at the end of days (as did the Apocalyptists in general). Jesus' Resurrection was understood as the beginning, or first event, signaling that the general resurrection was in progress. Paul thought the end would come in the lifetime of the members of his churches.[18] There was a tremendous apocalyptic tension in the New Testament consciousness anticipating the time of redemption. The Christian church has obviously had to modify the apocalyptic timetable. If Jesus' Resurrection was the first resurrection of one of the faithful, a long time has intervened before the remainder of the faithful are raised bodily to life. A number of theological strategies have been developed to deal with this problem. None is true to the New Testament expectation.

HS: Does the Qumrân material cast any light on the historicity of Jesus' Resurrection?

FMC: I don't think so. I don't see how it could. A scholar or two has argued that Qumrân had the notion of a resurrected Teacher of Righteousness. I think this view is based on faulty philology.

HS: What is the resurrection text from Qumrân?

FMC: I suspect you are referring to the text labeled 4Q521, which speaks of the dead being revivified—literally "made alive," which would be the normal way of speaking of resurrection.

HS: We have many instances of that in the Hebrew Bible, in subsequent Jewish literature and in the New Testament, so that would be nothing new.

FMC: References to resurrection in the sectarian literature from Qumrân are interesting because another way of speaking of eternal life is frequently used, especially life on the (heavenly) height with the angels. One can compare the mixture of language in the New Testament—life in "the bosom of Abraham," "eternal life" and "resurrection of the body."

HS: You said earlier that New Testament scholars haven't paid enough attention to the Qumrân material, something that I have noted also. I think it was Yigael Yadin who suggested that this is because they are so much more conversant with Greek than Semitic languages. They would have to learn a whole new discipline to pursue research in the field of Qumrân studies.

FMC: I think it is true that few New Testament scholars trained in the last generation have the tools to deal firsthand with the new manuscript discoveries. There are not only Semitic languages to be learned—notably Hebrew and Aramaic and, ideally, Ethiopic and Ugaritic—but also related paleographic and epigraphic disciplines. Some knowledge of the early rabbinic literature is also requisite. All this is added to the immense world of Greek literature, history and archaeology, the normal stuff of the training of New Testament scholars. Further, in recent years with the coming to light of the Nag Hammadi library, a discovery on the same order of magnitude as the Dead Sea Scrolls, Coptic and Gnostic studies have become necessary supplements to Greek studies for New Testament scholars.

The tradition of New Testament scholarship in the past generation has been dominated both in Germany and in America by the school of Rudolf Bultmann. He was, in the first instance, a great classicist, and the training of his students reflected his interests. Little attention was given to Semitic backgrounds of the New Testament. Theologically, too, Bultmann was open to the charge of Marcionism, a perennial heresy of the church, namely denigrating the Old Testament as belonging to the history of religion rather than treating it as Scripture on a par with the New Testament and an equal part of the canon. These factors worked together to leave New Testament scholars largely unprepared to participate in scroll research. There are, of course, exceptions. The late Morton Smith was one. K. G. Kuhn in Germany was another.

HS: What about Joseph Fitzmyer and Raymond Brown?

FMC: Fitzmyer and Brown certainly should be included. However, they are unusual in having taken degrees in Semitic languages under W. F. Albright in addition to pursuing New Testament studies. Fitzmyer has carried on research in Aramaic and Aramaic epigraphy all of his life. John Strugnell took degrees in both classics and Semitic languages. This is the ideal way for a New Testament scholar to prepare. I do not think, however, that this is the way future New Testament scholars will be trained. Rather I think in the future we will see increased specialization—the New Testament in a Jewish context, the New Testament in a Greek context, the New Testament and the early church (including Gnostic studies), New Testament archaeology. Generalists who can control, in some measure, all of these fields will be rare indeed.

HS: It seems to me that there is a confluence of specialties necessary for the study of the New Testament. In the past, illumination of the New Testament came primarily from studying Hellenistic Greek civilization. The focus is now shifting to Semitic parallels and the Semitic context for understanding the New Testament. Qumrân has led New Testament scholarship back to its Semitic background.

FMC: Not sufficiently in my opinion. New Testament scholars have been slow to integrate Qumrân literature into New Testament research. But the pendulum is swinging.

HS: Will the pendulum swing too far? After all, Greek elements did penetrate Christianity. We would be happier if Paul were late. In fact, he was a very early figure. Pauline epistles are the earliest New Testament documents. You cannot deny the Hellenistic Greek element in Paul. Isn't that true?

FMC: I should not wish to deny Hellenistic influences on New Testament literature, thought and institutions. But I am not sure

I would choose Paul as the most Hellenistic figure in the New Testament. He was a good Pharisee. Moreover, I believe there are Hellenistic influences even in the Qumrân literature. Doron Mendels, a classical historian at the Hebrew University in Jerusalem, has published an excellent paper analyzing how the discipline of the Qumrân community—celibacy, the sharing of wealth, the ideal of the communion of the group—is heavily influenced by Greek utopian literature.[19] Further, the Pharisaic party is by no means free of Greek influence. In fact, Greek influence was impossible to escape.

The whole of Syria-Palestine in this period was steeped in Hellenism, its influence ubiquitous, even in the discourse of those who resisted it. In the last two centuries before the fall of Jerusalem, about 20 percent of the Jewish ossuaries bear Greek graffiti, 40 percent Hebrew and 40 percent Aramaic, evidence, as I once argued, that most educated citizens of Jerusalem were trilingual, speaking Hebrew, Aramaic and Greek. The Hebrew language, in its loan-words and calques, shows Greek contacts. An interesting example of a calque, a loan (meaning from a similar word in another language), is the shift in the range of meaning of the word *ôlām*, meaning "eternity," "long duration, past or future," in the Hebrew Bible and early Hellenistic Jewish literature. The word came to have not only temporal meaning, but also the spatial meaning of "world," a meaning borrowed from Greek *aiōn*, meaning *both* "eternity" and "world." Hence *melek ôlām* means "eternal king" in the Hebrew Bible, but *melek hā ôlām* means "king of the world" in Jewish liturgy. Such calques and loans reflect widespread bilingualism.

HS: That raises the question of whether or not the Greek Hellenistic element entered Christianity via Hellenized Judaism or from Greek sources directly.

FMC: I should argue that in the Christian church in Jerusalem, and in the earliest strands of the New Testament, Hellenistic influences were largely inherited from Hellenized Judaism. Once one moves to the post-70 C.E. period, there is much more direct Greek influence from such currents as stoicism and late Platonism—for example, in the thought of a Jewish figure like Philo.

HS: What about Paul? Did the Hellenistic elements in Paul come from a Jewish context or from the Greek world?

FMC: I think the elements of Greek thought or culture in Paul come largely from his Hellenistic-Jewish background. He was a Pharisee of Pharisees, he brags.[20] On the other hand, he was a learned man who wrote Greek with tolerable ease (but not elegantly), and he was proud of his Roman citizenship, which few Jews possessed.

HS: The Qumrân materials have not been used much to expand our knowledge of Paul or to trace influences in his letters. But the Qumrân documents do enlighten us about what we thought was pure Greek thought in the Gospel of John.

FMC: The Gospel of John is a salient case of the importance of the Qumrân literature for understanding the complexity of Judaism in the period of Christian origins. We should have been warned. The Greek of John is awkward, transparently Hebrew in diction and syntax and idiom. In the case of Paul, much more can be done to understand his writings using the Qumrân literature. But note that members of the Pauline church share goods in common. Where does this communal, not to say communistic, element come from? The Pauline church also had a celibate ideal. These are themes little developed in wealthy Protestant churches, but they are found in Paul, as they are in the community of Essenes.

HS: Isn't there a christological element in Paul that you can not really trace to Jewish sources?

FMC: I am not sure that is true. Paul's development of the role of the Messiah as the new Adam with cosmological functions might be singled out, but this is a matter of stress rather than a truly novel development.

HS: Paul is very anti-halakhic. He has an exclusive devotion to faith.

FMC: Paul's position on the law is more complicated, though you have expressed a view shared by radical interpreters of Paul. To quote from 1 Corinthians, "So faith, hope, and love abide, these three; but the greatest of these is love." Here Paul echoes the *Shema* prayer as well as sayings of both Jesus and the rabbis when asked to summarize the law. Paul does reject the Law with a capital *L*, law as a mythical structure enslaving mankind.

HS: Why do you say a mythical structure?

FMC: By a mythical structure, I mean that which is divinely revealed and arbitrary, lowered perfect from heaven, which, therefore, cannot be altered or broken. Law in this sense condemns man if it means he must fulfill the law to achieve salvation. Paul's view of "fallen man" is such that he believes no one can fulfill the law in the law's radical intent (as opposed to outward observance). For the gentiles, Paul says, the Law (with a capital) is not for you. He is referring to the observance of dietary laws, sacrificial laws, purity laws, circumcision. From a conservative Jewish point of view (held by most of Paul's Jewish-Christian contemporaries), this meant a rejection of halakhic Judaism.

In Paul's letters, however, following his exposition of faith and reconciliation with God as the basis of salvation, he in effect brings back the law in a new, nonmythological mode. He urges his congregations to fulfill the moral teachings of the Hebrew Bible. He holds the Ten Commandments to be binding.[21] He stresses the great commandment that one should love his neighbor as himself.[22] He presumes that the Jews (including Jewish Christians) will continue their halakhic life. He does not reject Jews who refuse to be absorbed into the new branch of Judaism (that is, Christianity—a term which would be anachronistic on Paul's lips). He himself continues to go to the Temple. In Romans 11, he asserts that Israel continues to be the elect of God.

HS: If grafted back.

FMC: Paul argues that in the last days the alien grafted branch (the gentile Christian community) and Israel will become one. The natural branches will "be grafted back into their own olive tree." But Paul says plainly that Israel continues to be the elect of God. "...but as regards his [Israel's] election, they are beloved for the sake of their forefathers. For the gifts and the call of God are irrevocable."

The Pauline corpus of letters, however, is not as richly elucidated by the new literature from Qumrân as is the Johannine corpus or the Gospels.

HS: What about John the Baptist? Did he live at Qumrân at some time in his life?

FMC: My answer will not be satisfactory. When it is suggested to me that either Jesus or John the Baptist lived for some time at Qumrân, I have to reply that we have insufficient evidence to answer either yes or no. If the questioner replies, "Well, they both reflect a great deal of the kind of thought that you find in the Qumrân community. Isn't that best explained if they were there?" Again, I must reply that Essene communities were spread throughout Judea, Qumrân being only a "mother" community of leaders. Further, John and Jesus lived in a small country, and the apocalyptic currents of the day, religious and halakhic debates and controversies, strife between the several parties of Judaism, were in the air they breathed. I think we have to assume that John and Jesus, both teachers, were up on what was going on in the religious realm. Certainly in their main ministries, neither John nor Jesus was part of the Qumrân community or the Essene sect.

Take another case. Josephus claims to have spent years in the Essene community, presumably at Qumrân. Yet his writings show him to be a good Pharisee with no influence from Qumrân. Even his description of the Essenes is plagiarized from an older source.[23] Would one argue then that Josephus was never at Qumrân or that he never studied Qumrân traditions or literature?

HS: He doesn't say he was at Qumrân, does he?

FMC: No, he says he submitted himself to "hard training and exercise" when he investigated each of the three parties of Judaism—the Pharisees, Sadducees and Essenes. He also tells us that he spent three years in the wilderness as a disciple of a certain Bannus.

HS: What about John the Baptist? You do have him recorded as being in geographical proximity to Qumrân.

FMC. Well he goes down to the Jordan. Qumrân is not at the Jordan.

HS: He's out in the wilderness, though.

FMC: Yes, in order to baptize in the Jordan. Perhaps the Essenes too used the Jordan for baptism; they were baptists. No, really all we can say is that his thought was apocalyptic and had much in common with the apocalyptic eschatology of the Qumrân literature. However, the New Testament pictures him as leading his own movement. If he was an Essene, he broke with the movement. We should say much the same thing about Jesus. If he once was part of the Essene movement, he broke with it (as well as with John) and pursued his own way.

HS: Let's talk a little bit about the area of the Dead Sea. There were lots of sites there, not just Qumrân: ʿÊn Feshkha, Khirbet Mazin, etc.

FMC: The installation at ʿÊn Feshkha was an agricultural adjunct to Qumrân. The pottery at the site was made in the same kiln as the pottery of Qumrân, and the structures, agricultural and technical, complement the settlement at Khirbet Qumrân. There are a number of sites in the Buqêʿah above Qumrân and along the shore south of Qumrân and north of ʿÊn Gedi from the seventh century B.C.E. The three Buqêʿah sites are paramilitary sites with adjacent farms discovered by Milik and me in 1954; the late Pesach Bar-Adon added four small coastal sites. One ruin seems to have been a port.

HS: Khirbet Mazin at the mouth of the Kidron?

FMC: I was thinking rather of the site to the north of Qumrân identified by Bar-Adon as Beth Arabah.

HS: There was a fair amount of maritime commerce on the Dead Sea, wasn't there?

FMC: Yes, some no doubt. Trade in bitumen, salt and probably balm may have traveled north by water; and at the Lisân there was a ford in Roman times across the Dead Sea.

MUSHROOM-LIKE SALT FORMATIONS sprout from the Dead Sea, known in ancient literature as the Salt Sea. Remarkably high saline levels here prevent all but microscopic life forms from flourishing. The Qumrân community on the northwest shore overlooks the Dead Sea.

HS: So the wilderness of the Dead Sea was not so isolated.

FMC. Nothing can be really isolated in such a small country. The Buqêʿah sites are 15 miles from Jerusalem. However, several years ago an American bishop, Bishop Pike, died of dehydration trying to walk out of the Buqêʿah after his vehicle stalled. Population in the wilderness of Judea was sparse in the seventh century when the small paramilitary forts were built and even sparser in the Hellenistic-Roman period when the Essene community at Qumrân and ʿÊn Feshkha flourished. Hence the need for fortifications. They were vulnerable to raids from the Edomite south and from bedouin razzias (raids by camel riders). This menace is nicely documented in the seventh- and sixth-century ostraca from ʿArad.[24]

HS: What about de Vaux's idea that Qumrân was a monastic community?

FMC: If I am not mistaken, de Vaux carefully avoided calling the Qumrân community center a monastery. He was a historian aware of the origins of the monastic movement. But a number of scholars have called the community center a monastery. The whole notion is completely anachronistic. Recent revisionist arguments that the site is, in effect, a hacienda are, in my opinion (and yours, I think), also nonsense. The architecture of the site, notably the great pantry with its vast quantity of common pottery made at the site evidently for use at the communal meals, fits best with the interpretation of the site as an Essene community center. Most of the members lived in caves outside, and the center boasted a scriptorium and a banquet hall, in short, communal facilities but limited living quarters. The argument that the remains of the site do not indicate abject poverty, and hence the site is not the Essene center, actually assumes the monastic paradigm for the Essene community. But although the community shared property in common, poverty was only theoretical. The structure of the community is very close to that of the early church and to the Pharisaic *ḥabûrôt*, as described by the late Saul Lieberman.[25]

HS: How do you account for the enormous library associated with this settlement?

FMC: There can be no doubt, I think, that the community consisted of an intellectual elite. Their discipline required a 24-hour regimen of studying Torah, which we understand as what became the Hebrew Bible and the broader literature of the apocalyptic movement, which was later rejected for the canon. They studied, we are told, in eight-hour shifts.

They obviously had a thriving scriptorium. This is not only based on the evidence of ink pots and putative plaster desks for copying documents. It is the only explanation, I think, for the fact that a small group of scribes wrote a large number of the documents that survived in the caves. The scribe of the Rule of the Community from Cave 1, for example, copied a Samuel manuscript from Cave 4, entered

THE SCRIPTORIUM. This long, narrow room is thought by many scholars to have been the center of Qumrân scribal activities. Excavators uncovered remains of three plastered mudbrick tables or chairs, a low bench and several inkwells. According to the most widely held theory, scribes copied works that were read aloud to them.

Pauline Donceel-Voûte and Robert Donceel, who are currently completing the final excavation report of the site, disagree. In keeping with their view that Qumrân was a winter villa rather than a religious community, they believe that an upper story of this room was a Roman-style *triclinium*, or dining room.

corrections in the great Isaiah Scroll from Cave 1 and copied the Testimonia List from Cave 4. It is unlikely that these miscellaneous manuscripts came from the outside. Further, the earliest manuscripts are written in distinctive hands, never repeated in other manuscripts. These were almost certainly imported into the community. Exemplars from a sectarian library come from the 11 caves in close proximity to Qumrân along with domestic wares baked at Qumrân. The mass of the library is from Cave 4 under the marl terrace that supports the ruin of the community center.

An even more impressive argument that the library belonged to the people who occupied the center and the surrounding caves is the curve made by the dates of manuscripts. The great mass of manuscripts begins about 150 or 140 B.C.E., increases in number in the next century and tails off toward 70 C.E. The archaeological record of the site follows the same pattern. In short the archaeological chronology and the paleographic chronology are effectively identical. It is too much to suppose that this is by chance.

I am reminded of an episode when my grandson was left alone in the kitchen with instructions not to drink more Hawaiian Punch. His father was called out of the kitchen to the telephone, and when he returned, Nathaniel was sitting, still alone, with an empty bottle of punch. His father asked rhetorically, "Did you drink that punch?"

POTTERY FROM QUMRÂN. The scrolls from Cave 1 were discovered in tall storage jars like the one shown here on the right. The unusual shape suggests that jars like this may have been made especially for storing manuscripts. Excavations at the Qumrân settlement yielded other vessels similar to the ones in which the scrolls were found. The pottery and the linen in which the scrolls were wrapped (the latter were dated by carbon 14 tests), as well as the writing style, all combined to date the scrolls to the last two centuries B.C.E. and the first century C.E.

Nathaniel hesitated and said, "Well, it is possible." I find the same level of possibility that the sectarian library belonged to the sectarian community of Qumrân.

I should not argue that all the sectarian documents found in the library were composed at Qumrân. As I have stressed, members of the party or sect came from all parts of Judea if we are to believe the testimony of Josephus and the evidence of the Damascus Document.

HS: Do you think the main Essene library in Jerusalem might have been brought to this Essene desert enclave when Jerusalem was threatened by the Romans?

FMC: The community was destroyed in 68 C.E. by the forces of Vespasian and Trajan when he reduced Jericho, before he marched against Jerusalem.[26]

HS: But the Essenes may not have known that in 66 when the war began.

FMC: If so, they had poor intelligence. At any event, the persecution of the leaders of the Essene movement by the priestly rulers in Jerusalem, the occasion we are told for their flight into the desert, is a more plausible reason for the establishment of a library at Qumrân. Further they could not have pursued their rigorous discipline of Torah study and biblical exposition without a library and a scriptorium. Finally, I repeat my argument that the dates of the series of manuscripts follows the pattern of the archaeological chronology of the community center.

HS: What is your explanation for the library being split up?

FMC: I think it is clear from the finds in the caves associated with the manuscripts that the caves were living quarters. Except for Cave 4, relatively few manuscripts were left in the caves. Cave 4 was the primary depository of a huge library of which some 600 fragmentary manuscripts survived. I think the few manuscripts found in most of the caves were borrowed from the main collection by individuals who lived in the caves to pursue private study. The scrolls were abandoned there; they were not "hidden." Only in Cave 1 were the scrolls in jars, and storage jars were a normal place to keep manuscripts in this period. I think Cave 4 is the main library of Qumrân, and the scrolls were left helter-skelter on the floor of Cave 4, neither hidden nor protected.

HS: There is an enormous interest on the part of the general public in the scrolls. They are fascinated with them. Some scholars have said that they are not that important. Robert Alter (professor of Hebrew and comparative literature at the University of California, Berkeley) said that in Commentary. *William Dever (professor of Near Eastern archaeology at the University of Arizona) agrees. And the texts are often esoteric. Why should the public, the man in the street, be interested in the scrolls?*

FMC: I am tempted to answer that the general public has better judgment than either Alter or Dever. I don't think it is possible to overstate the importance of this library. I should agree with those who express disdain for the scrolls only to the extent that I think much of the public excitement about the scrolls is for the wrong reasons, stirred up by the tabloid press that speaks irresponsibly about threats to the faith of Jews and Christians and prints stories about conspiracies created out of whole cloth.

The scrolls of the Jordan Rift, from Qumrân, Dâliyeh and the southern caves, must be called collectively the greatest archaeological discovery of all times. The documents come from the crucial period in the emergence of Western civilization when Christianity came into being and normative Judaism crystallized, the two great religious traditions that, combined with the heritage of Greek thought and logic, shaped our philosophic, religious and moral self-understanding. A comparable discovery would be the recovery of the great library of Alexandria.

It is too bad that there are no straight historical works among the scrolls. They are virtually all religious documents with historical allusions usually hidden in esoteric language. Still it is hard to imagine a more important discovery. For the religious person, at least in my Calvinist tradition, a primary obligation is to worship God with the intellect. And since our religion is historical, whether Jewish or Christian, we are obliged necessarily to be concerned with the history of our religious traditions. The more light we can shed on crucial moments in the history of our religious community (or on the birth of Western culture to speak more broadly), the better. The longer and more precise our memory is, the more civilized we are. The scrolls are obviously of great import to the world of the church and synagogue. The light they shed on a critical period in human history should also make all academicians and lovers of humane letters exult.

ENDNOTES

Opening Conversation

1. Frank Moore Cross, "William Foxwell Albright: Orientalist," *Bulletin of the American Schools of Oriental Research* (*BASOR*) 200 (1970), pp. 7-11.

Chapter 1, Israelite Origins

1. The Epic tradition, as referred to by Professor Cross, is the combined JE strand of the Pentateuch. Scholars divide the Pentateuch into four principal authorial strands: J for the Yahwist (Jahwist in German) because Yahweh is the customary appellation of God in this strand; E for the Elohist because Elohim or a form of that name is the customary appellation of God in this strand; P for the Priestly code; and D for the Deuteronomist. J and E were combined at an early date. Professor Cross and some other scholars also have detected first and second editions of D. Finally, the whole was put together by a redactor often referred to as R.—**Ed.**

2. Eduard Meyer, *Geschichte des Altertums* (Stuttgart and Berlin: J.G. Cottäsche Buchhandlung Nachfolger, 1921).

3. See the plaintive remarks of Rudolph Cohen in "Did I Excavate Kadesh-Barnea?" *Biblical Archaeology Review* (*BAR*) 7:3 (1981), and his desperate suggestion of dating Mosaic traditions toward the end of the third millennium (*sic!*) in "The Mysterious MB I People— Does the Exodus Tradition in the Bible Preserve the Memory of Their Entry into Canaan?" *BAR* 9:2 (1983).

4. See Peter J. Parr et al., "Preliminary Survey in N.W. Arabia, 1968," *Bulletin of the Institute of Archaeology* 8-9: 1968-1969 (1970), pp. 193-242, 10 (1972), pp. 23-61; Parr, "Contacts Between Northwest Arabia and Jordan in the Late Bronze and Iron Ages," in *Studies in the History and Archaeology of Jordan*, ed. A. Hadidi (Amman: Department of Antiquities, 1982), pp. 127-134; M.L. Ingraham, T.J. Johnson, B. Rihani and I. Shatla, "Saudi Arabian Comprehensive Survey Program: Preliminary Report on a Reconnaissance Survey of the Northwestern Province," *Atla* 5 (1981), pp. 59-84.

5. For more on the Mesha Stele, see Siegfried Horn, "Why the Moabite Stone Was Blown to Pieces," *BAR* 12:6 (1986).

6. Located, I have argued, near the waterfall in the present-day valley of ʿUyun Musa (the Springs of Moses), the biblical "valley over against Beth Peor."

7. Martin Noth, "Die Wallfahrsweg zum Sinai," *Palästina Jahrbuch* 36 (1940), pp. 5-28; cf. Cross, *Canaanite Myth and Hebrew Epic: Essays in the History of the Religion of Israel* (Cambridge, MA: Harvard University Press, 1973), pp. 308-317.

8. See Ze'ev Meshel, "Did Yahweh Have a Consort?" *BAR* 5:2 (1979), and André Lemaire, "Who or What Was Yahweh's Asherah?" *BAR* 10:6 (1984).

9. See Deuteronomy 2:1. The "Red Sea" here and in Numbers 14:25 (as well as in 1 Kings 9:26 and Jeremiah 49:21) is certainly a reference to the Gulf of Aqaba, as is generally recognized by critical scholars. See, for example, Noth, *Numbers: A Commentary* (Philadelphia: Westminster Press, 1968), p. 110.

10. For the linguistic evidence, see Cross, "Reuben, Firstborn of Jacob," *Zeitschrift für die alttestamentliche Wissenschaft* 100 (1988), supplement, *Lebenndige Forschung im Alten Testament*, p. 63 n. 54.

11. For those interested in reading more, there is a new, magisterial edition of these letters by William L. Moran, *Les lettres d'El Amarna*, trans. Dominique Collon and Henri Cazelles (Paris: Les Editions du Cerf, 1987). See now *The Amarna Letters*, ed. Moran (Baltimore: Johns Hopkins University Press, 1992).

12. See Bernhard W. Anderson, "Mendenhall Disavows Paternity," *Bible Review (BR)* 2:2 (1986).

13. Norman K. Gottwald, "Were the Early Israelites Pastoral Nomads?" *BAR* 4:2 (1978); see also "Israel's Emergence in Canaan—BR Interviews Norman Gottwald," *BR* 5:5 (1989).

14. See Israel Finkelstein, *The Archaeology of the Israelite Settlement* (Jerusalem: Israel Exploration Society, 1988).

15. One need only examine the problems of fragments of tradition in Judges chapter one.

16. See A.M. Khazanov (*Nomads and the Outside World*, trans. J. Crookenden [Cambridge, UK: Cambridge University Press, 1983], esp. p. 152), who asserts that "confederations" among nomads "in all circumstances...emerge for military-political reasons."

17. For the date of early portions of the hymn and the translation I quote below, see Theodore Hiebert, *God of My Victory: The Ancient Hymn in Habakkuk 3*, Harvard Semitic Monographs 38 (Atlanta: Scholars Press, 1986).

18. See the Priestly portions of Numbers 25 (25:6-18) and Numbers 31.

19. For a brief exposition of my analysis of the so-called Epic sources, JE, see Cross, "The Epic Traditions of Early Israel: Epic Narrative and the Reconstruction of Early Israelite Institutions," in *The Poet and the Historian*, ed. Richard E. Friedman, Harvard Semitic Studies 26 (Chico, CA: Scholars Press, 1983), pp. 13-39.

20. I have discussed these conflict stories in detail and their origin in the conflict between two priestly houses in the chapter "The Priestly Houses of Early Israel" in *Canaanite Myth*, pp. 193-215.

21. Cross, "Reuben, Firstborn of Jacob."

22. "The sons of Reuben the firstborn of Israel (for he was the firstborn; but because he polluted his father's couch, his birthright was given to the sons of Joseph the son of Israel, so that he is not enrolled in the genealogy according to the birthright; though Judah became strong among his brothers and a prince was from him, yet the birthright belonged to Joseph)..." (1 Chronicles 5:1-2).

Chapter 2, Israelite Religion

1. David Noel Freedman and Cross, *Studies in Ancient Yahwistic Poetry*, Society of Biblical Literature Dissertation Ser. 21 (Missoula, MT: Scholars Press/Society of Biblical Literature, 1975).

2. A long exposition and documentation of the languages of revelation in the Hebrew Bible can be found in the chapter "The Storm Theophany in the Bible" in Cross, *Canaanite Myth*, pp. 156-194.

3. I am indebted to Professor Lawrence Stager for this information.

4. The best treatment of the stele and its implications for Israel's occupation of the land is, in my opinion, the paper by Lawrence E. Stager, "Merneptah, Israel and Sea Peoples: New Light on an Old Relief," *Eretz-Israel* 18 (1985), pp. 56*-64*; see also Frank J. Yurco, "3,200-Year-Old Picture of Israelites Found in Egypt," *BAR* 15:5 (1990).

5. Note that Amos' oracle here quoted includes these words about the usual practice of religion: "I hate, I despise your feasts,/ And I will take no delight in your sacred assemblies./ Yea, though you offer me holocausts [burnt offerings] and your meal offerings,/ I will not accept them;/ Neither will I regard/ the communion offerings of your fat beasts./ Take away from me the noise of your hymns;/ And let me not hear the melody of your stringed instruments./ But let justice well up as waters…" (Amos 5:21-24).

6. See Cross and Freedman, "An Inscribed Jar Handle from Raddana," *BASOR* 201 (1971), pp. 19-22.

7. On occasion a god may be restricted to the underworld, or Yamm, deified sea, may be banned from dry ground. But even then, Ba'al is resurrected from the dead (and confinement to the underworld), and the cosmic waters may break out of their bounds and bring a flood.

8. The masculine or patriarchal language used in describing God in the Bible offends many. At least one should note, however, that Israel's deity is without a female counterpart and, in contrast to the gods in central myths of sacral marriage in the ancient Near East, he engages in no sexual activity. In reality a god without a spouse is sexless.

9. Cross, *Canaanite Myth*, p. viii.

Chapter 3, Alphabet

1. The Egyptians attributed the XVth and XVIth dynasties to the Hyksos. "Hyksos" is a rendering of an Egyptian term for "foreign ruler." The Hyksos ruled in the 18th and the first half of the 17th centuries B.C.E.

2. Sir Alan Gardiner, in his famous paper of 1915, "The Egyptian Origin of the Alphabet" (*Journal of Egyptian Archaeology* 3 [1916], pp. 1-16), attributed the inscriptions to the XIIth Dynasty, which came to an end in the early 18th century B.C.E.

3. Flinders Petrie was the most famous of the founders of Palestinian archaeology. He also dug in Egypt and Sinai.

4. William F. Albright, "The Early Alphabetic Inscriptions from Sinai and Their Decipherment," *BASOR* 110 (1948), pp. 6-22; and Itzhak Beit-Arieh, "Serabit el-Khadim: New Metallurgical and Chronological Aspects," *Levant* 17 (1985), pp. 89-116.

5. The earliest inscriptions with hard dates (late 16th century) are those published by Joe D. Seger, "The Gezer Jars Signs: New Evidence of the Earliest Alphabet," in *The Word of the Lord Shall Go Forth: Essays in Honor of David Noel Freedman in Celebration of His Sixtieth Birthday*, ed. Carol L. Meyers and M. O'Connor (Winona Lake, IN: Eisenbrauns/American Schools of Oriental Research, 1983), pp. 477-495.

6. The Amarna tablets—found at Tell el-Amarna in Egypt—are written in Akkadian cuneiform, the lingua franca of diplomatic correspondence in the 14th century B.C.E. between Egypt and Egyptian vassals in Syria-Palestine, as well as between the great powers—Egypt, the Hittite kingdom, Mitanni and Mesopotamia.

7. Cross, "Newly Discovered Inscribed Arrowheads of the 11th Century B.C.E.," *Israel Museum Journal* 10 (1992), pp. 57-62; and "An Inscribed Arrowhead of the Eleventh Century B.C.E. in the Bible Lands Museum in Jerusalem," *Eretz-Israel* 23 (1992), pp. 21-26.

8. See Cross, "An Interpretation of the Nora Stone," *BASOR* 208 (1972), p. 19; and "Leaves from an Epigraphist's Notebook," *Catholic Biblical Quarterly* 36 (1974), pp. 486-494. These two papers are reprinted in *Studies in Sardinian Archaeology*, ed. Miriam S. Balmuth and R.J. Rowland (Ann Arbor: University of Michigan Press, 1982), pp. 53-66. More recently, see Cross, "Phoenicians in the West," in *Studies in Sardinian Archaeology II: Sardinia in the Mediterranean*, ed. Balmuth (Ann Arbor: University of Michigan Press, 1986), pp. 116-130; and "The Oldest Phoenician Inscription from Sardinia: The Fragmentary Stele from Nora," in *"Working With No Data": Semitic and Egyptian Studies Presented to Thomas O. Lambdin*, ed. David M. Golomb (Winona Lake, IN: Eisenbrauns, 1987), pp. 65-74. For a different dating of the Nora inscription, see Edward Lipinski, "Epigraphy in Crisis," *BAR* 16:4 (1990).

9. The most influential defender of this late date was Rhys Carpenter; see his "The Antiquity of the Greek Alphabet," *American Journal of Archaeology* 37 (1933), pp. 8-29. The discovery of Phrygian inscriptions (a daughter script of Greek) from Gordion dating to the middle and second half of the eighth century renders the seventh-century date impossible. Rhys Carpenter dated the development of the Phrygian script from the Greek *after* 600.

10. Martin Bernal's attempt to place the transmission of the alphabet to the Aegean before 1400 B.C.E. I believe to be without merit; see his *Cadmean Letters: The Transmission of the Alphabet to the Aegean and Further West Before 1400 B.C.* (Winona Lake, IN: Eisenbrauns, 1992).

11. See Albright, "Neglected Factors in the Greek Intellectual Revolution," *Proceedings of the American Philosophical Society* 116 (1972), pp. 225-242.

12. We label the seventh-century Deuteronomist DTR_1, the Exilic Deuteronomist DTR_2. The former was a propaganda work of the late seventh-century court of Josiah, reviewing Israel's history in order to motivate the reform of Josiah. The latter retouches Deuteronomy and the Deuteronomistic history in the interests of transforming it into an elaborate sermon justifying Israel's exile, underlining Israel's breach of covenant and apostasy, and defending the justice and sovereignty of Israel's God.

Chapter 4, Seals

1. Cross, "The Tabernacle: A Study from an Archaeological and Historical Approach," *Biblical Archaeologist* 10 (1947), pp. 45-68.

Chapter 5, Dead Sea Scrolls

1. Albright, "A Biblical Fragment from the Maccabaean Age: The Nash Papyrus," *Journal of Biblical Literature* 56 (1937), pp. 145-176.

2. The Wrathful Lion is found in an interpretation of Nahum 2:12-14 in the Commentary on Nahum (4Q169 1.5-6) and probably refers to Alexander Jannaeus. The False Oracle is a title taken from Micah 2:11 and is regularly combined with Ezekiel 13:8-12 in sectarian exegesis, for example, in the Commentary on Habakkuk (1QpHab 10:9-13). The Cursed Man or Man of Belial is found in a quotation from the sectarian Psalms of Joshua alluding to Joshua 6:26 found in the Testimonia document (4Q175: lines 21-30).

3. I refer to a title in so-called Pseudo-Daniel[d] (4Q246 2:1) alluding to Psalm 2:7 and 2 Samuel 7:14. See now Émile Puech, "Fragment d'une apocalypse en araméen (4Q246 = pseudo-Dan[d]) et le 'royaume de Dieu,'" *Revue biblique* 99 (1992), pp. 98-131.

4. George Foot Moore, *Judaism in the First Centuries of the Christian Era: The Age of the Tannaim*, 3 vols. (Cambridge, MA: Harvard University Press, 1962), vol. 1, pp. 126-128.

5. James M. Robinson, *A New Quest of the Historical Jesus*, Studies in Biblical Theology 25 (London: SCM Press, 1959), p. 32 (recent edition, Philadelphia: Fortress Press, 1983).

6. Helmut Koester, *Introduction to the New Testament*, vol. 1, *History, Culture and Religion of the Hellenistic Age* (Philadelphia: Fortress Press, 1982), p. 230.

7. Klaus Baltzer, *The Covenant Formulary in Old Testament, Jewish, and Early Christian Writings* (Philadelphia: Fortress Press, 1971).

8. Cross, "A New Qumran Biblical Fragment Related to the Original Hebrew Underlying the Septuagint," *BASOR* 132 (1953), pp. 15-26.

9. Sanballaṭ is mentioned in Nehemiah 2:10,19, 3:33, 4:1, 6:1,2,5,12,14, 13:28.

10. The figure of $105,000 is given by Yadin in his popular volume on the Temple Scroll (*The Temple Scroll* [New York: Random House, 1985], p. 43) and in his monumental three-volume edition of the scroll (*The Temple Scroll* [Jerusalem: Israel Exploration Society, 1983], vol. 1, p. 4).

11. John M. Allegro (with A.A. Anderson), *Qumrân Cave 4,I (4Q158-4Q186)*, Discoveries in the Judaean Desert 5 (Oxford: Clarendon Press, 1968).

12. John Strugnell, "Notes en marge du volume V des *Discoveries in the Judaean Desert of Jordan*," *Revue de Qumrân* 7:2 (1970), pp. 163-276.

13. See esp. 2 Samuel 7:14; Psalms 2:7.

14. See, for example, Isaiah 25:6-8; Isaiah 55:1-5.

15. *Die keilalphabetischen Texte aus Ugarit* 1.96.3-5.

16. Gershon Scholem, *The Messianic Idea in Judaism* (New York: Schocken Books, 1971), pp. 8-9.

17. For example, the pericope on the valley of dry bones in Ezekiel 37.

18. See, for example, 1 Corinthians 7:29-31, 15:51; Romans 13:11-12.

19. Doron Mendels, "Hellenistic Utopia and the Essenes," *Harvard Theological Review* 72 (1979), pp. 207-222.

20. See Philippians 3:4-6; cf. Galatians 1:13-14.

21. See, for example, 1 Corinthians 6:9-10; Galatians 5:16-21.

22. See, for example, Romans 13:8-10; cf. the hymn to love in 1 Corinthians 13:1-13, esp. 13:2.

23. See the discussion of sources in Morton Smith, "The Description of the Essenes in Josephus and the Philophumena," *Hebrew Union College Annual* 29 (1958), pp. 273-313.

24. See Yohanan Aharoni, *Arad Inscriptions: Judean Desert Studies* (Jerusalem: Israel Exploration Society, 1981), Ostraca 3, 21, and esp. 24 and 40.

25. Saul Lieberman, "The Discipline in the So-called Dead Sea Manual of Discipline," *Journal of Biblical Literature* 71 (1952), pp. 199-206.

26. See the discussion of the movements of the Roman legions in Cross, *The Ancient Library of Qumrân* (Garden City, NY: Anchor Books, 1961), pp. 62-63 n. 18.

GLOSSARY

ʿ**Apiru:** a group of people outside the mainstream of Canaanite society in the 14th to 13th centuries B.C.E., described in some ancient texts as mercenaries or outlaws; some scholars believe they were one component of the early Israelite confederation.

apotheosis: the elevation of a mortal to the status of a god; also, a glorified ideal.

Baʿal: the Canaanite storm god who, under the aegis of the father of the gods ʾEl), became regent of the cosmos. Baʿal means "lord"; his personal name was Haddu or Hadad.

boustrophedon: "as the ox ploughs"; an ancient method of writing in which the direction of written lines alternates between left to right and right to left or, more rarely, up and down.

collared-rim jars: tall storage jars with a capacity of 10 to 15 gallons with collar-like rims, widely used during Iron Age I (1200-1000 B.C.E.); most archaeologists believe this type of jar is characteristic of Israelite sites.

Docetism: the belief that Jesus appeared to be human but was, in fact, completely divine; a view opposed by the Council of Chalcedon in 451 C.E., which affirmed that Jesus was "truly God and truly man."

ʾ**El:** head of the Canaanite pantheon, the father of the gods and creator of heaven and earth.

epic: a literary term applied to poetry or prose on a large subject, such as the history of a people; Cross uses the term regarding the Bible and early Israelite literature to refer to traditions originating in oral narratives, especially poetic oral narratives. The great Greek and Hebrew epics characteristically give expression to the identity of a people, defining values, vocation and destiny.

eschatology: the doctrine of the end of days, including the consummation of history.

genizah: a storeroom for damaged, discarded or heretical manuscripts and sacred relics, usually attached to a synagogue.

Gnosticism: from the Greek *gnosis* (knowledge, wisdom); a religious movement that flourished in the first and second centuries C.E. based on the idea that a higher knowledge was given by God to the enlightened few; according to Gnostic thought, matter was evil, and spirit was good. A characteristic Gnostic belief was that the creator of the material world was evil.

henotheism: the belief in one god for one locale or people and other gods for other locales or peoples.

hierophant: an interpreter of sacred mysteries or esoteric principles.

monolatry: the worship of one god while believing that other gods exist.

onomasticon: an inventory of personal names and their use in a particular time and place.

ontology: the branch of metaphysics dealing with the nature of being.

palimpsest: a reused manuscript or papyrus on which a later writing was written over a more or less effaced earlier writing.

patronymic: the name of the father or ancestor, or a name derived from that of the father or ancestor, formed by adding an affix.

pictograph: a picture symbolizing a sound, syllable or a word.

siglum: a letter or symbol used to designate a particular text.

stele: an upright stone slab or pillar, frequently bearing an inscription or design or both.

syllabary: a catalogue of syllabic signs.

syllogistic reasoning: a logical argument that uses syllogisms; for example: All A is B; all B is C; therefore all A is C.

syncretism: the mixture or attempted reconciliation of diverse or opposite tenets or practices, especially in religion.

Tetrateuch: Genesis, Exodus, Leviticus and Numbers.

theomachy: conflict among the gods.

theophagy: a rite involving ingesting the flesh or blood of a god.

theophany: the manifestation of a god to a human.

theophoric names: names with a divine element.

tradent: the receiver, shaper and transmitter of tradition.

LIST OF ILLUSTRATIONS

Frank Moore Cross today, *Hershel Shanks*

Mesha Stele (Moabite Stone), *Erich Lessing*

Map, route of the Exodus

Camels in biblical Midian, *Peter Parr*

Map, tribal allotments according to the Book of Joshua

Remains of temple to Egyptian goddess Hathor, *Beno Rothenberg*

King Solomon's Pillars, Timna, *Beno Rothenberg*

Midianite pottery, Timna, *Beno Rothenberg*

Fortified citadel, Qurayyah, *Peter Parr*

Midianite ware, *Peter Parr*

Mount Nebo, *Jane Taylor/Sonia Halliday Photographs*

Pottery fragment showing Yahweh and ʾAsherah, *Photo: Avraham Hai;
    Drawing: Pirhiya Beck*

Kuntillet ʿAjrûd, *Zev Meshel*

Cuneiform tablet, Tell el-Amarna, *Staatliche Museen zu Berlin*

Warrior god Baʿal, stele from Ugarit, *National Museums, Paris*

Merneptah Stele, *Jürgen Liepe*

Inscribed jar handle, Raddana, *Joseph Callaway*

Chart, the development of ʾalep

Sumerian god Ninurta attacks dragon, shell inlay, *Avraham Hai/Bible
    Lands Museum, Jerusalem*

Hieroglyphic writing, wooden stele, *Oriental Institute, University of Chicago*

Picture writing, Sumerian stone tablet, *University of Pennsylvania Museum
    of Archaeology and Anthropology*

Cuneiform tablet, Ebla, *Erich Lessing*

Chart, Egyptian hieroglyphics and Semitic letters

Drawing, acrophonic principle

Inscribed arrowheads, *Zev Radovan/Bible Lands Museum, Jerusalem*

Egyptian mining site, Serābîṭ el-Khâdem, *Hershel Shanks*

Remains of temple to Hathor, Serābîṭ el-Khâdem, *Zev Radovan*

Proto-Sinaitic inscriptions, Serābîṭ el-Khâdem, *Hershel Shanks*

Inscription on stone plaque, Serābîṭ el-Khâdem, *Avraham Hai*

Drawing, piscine symbol on storage jar, *Joe Seger*

Early Greek inscription, boustrophedon style, *Frank Moore Cross*

Nora Fragment, *Frank Moore Cross*

Ammonite seal impression, Tell el-ʿUmeiri, *Photo and drawing courtesy
    of Larry Herr*

Samaria Papyrus 1, Wâdī ed-Dâliyeh, *Frank Moore Cross*

Bulla from Samaria papyri, *Frank Moore Cross*

Seal of Miqnêyaw, *Frank Moore Cross*

Nora Stone, *Frank Moore Cross*

Isaiah Scroll, Qumrân Cave 1, *John Trever*

Nash Papyrus, *By permission of the Syndics of Cambridge University*

Eliezer L. Sukenik, *Israel Museum, Jerusalem*

Abisha Scroll, *Plate XII,* Sefer Abisa, *by F. Castro*

MMT, the "Halakhic Epistle," *Israel Antiquities Authority*

Damascus Document, *Biblical Archaeology Society*

Damascus Document, fragments from Qumrân, *Israel Antiquities Authority*

Frank Moore Cross, entrance to Qumrân Cave 1, *Estate of John M. Allegro*

Qumrân Cave 4, *Hershel Shanks*

Cave 4, interior, *Weston Fields*

Qumrân settlement, aerial view, *Werner Braun*

Roland de Vaux, *Theodore A. Rosen*

G. Lankester Harding, with de Vaux and Jozef T. Milik, *Estate of John M. Allegro*

4QSam^a, *Israel Antiquities Authority*

William Foxwell Albright, *Biblical Archaeology Society*

Khalil Iskander Shahin (Kando), *Biblical Archaeology Society*

Palestine Archaeological Museum, *David Harris*

Elizabeth Hay Bechtel, *Jon H. Bechtel*

Paul Lapp, *Nancy Lapp*

Mughâret ʾAbū-Shinjeh, Wâdī ed-Dâliyeh, *Nancy Lapp*

Papyrus with seven seal impressions, Wâdī ed-Dâliyeh, *Frank Moore Cross*

Sanballaṭ seal impression, Wâdī ed-Dâliyeh, *Frank Moore Cross*

Yigael Yadin, *Werner Braun*

Jozef T. Milik, *Estate of John M. Allegro*

Jean Starcky, with Cross and Milik, *Frank Moore Cross*

John Strugnell, *Estate of John M. Allegro*

John M. Allegro, *Estate of John M. Allegro*

Son of God fragment, *Israel Antiquities Authority*

Salt formations, Dead Sea, *David Harris*

Scriptorium, Qumrân, *Zev Radovan*

Pottery, Qumrân, *David Harris*

INDEX

(Boldface numerals designate captions)